INTERNET THEORY, TECHNOLOGY AND APPLICATIONS

CYBERSPACE THREAT LANDSCAPE

OVERVIEW, RESPONSE AUTHORITIES, AND CAPABILITIES

INTERNET THEORY, TECHNOLOGY AND APPLICATIONS

Additional books in this series can be found on Nova's website under the Series tab.

Additional e-books in this series can be found on Nova's website under the e-book tab.

INTERNET THEORY, TECHNOLOGY AND APPLICATIONS

CYBERSPACE THREAT LANDSCAPE

OVERVIEW, RESPONSE AUTHORITIES, AND CAPABILITIES

CODY L. BARKER
EDITOR

nova publishers
New York

Library of Congress Cataloging-in-Publication Data

ISBN: 978-1-63482-338-8

Published by Nova Science Publishers, Inc. † New York

CONTENTS

PREFACE

This book provides an overview of cyberspace threats, and discusses cyber incident response practices.

Chapter 1 – Cyberspace is defined by the Department of Defense as a global domain consisting of the interdependent networks of information technology infrastructures and resident data, including the Internet, telecommunications networks, computer systems, and embedded processors and controllers. Attacks in cyberspace have seemingly been on the rise in recent years with a variety of participating actors and methods. As the United States has grown more reliant on information technology and networked critical infrastructure components, many questions arise about whether the nation is properly organized to defend its digital strategic assets. Cyberspace integrates the operation of critical infrastructures, as well as commerce, government, and national security. Because cyberspace transcends geographic boundaries, much of it is outside the reach of U.S. control and influence.

The Department of Homeland Security is the lead federal agency responsible for securing the nation's non-security related digital assets. The Department of Defense also plays a role in defense of cyberspace. The National Military Strategy for Cyberspace Operations instructs DOD to support the DHS, as the lead federal agency, in national incident response and support to other departments and agencies in critical infrastructure and key resources protection. DOD is responsible for defensive operations on its own information networks as well as the sector-specific agency for the defense of the Defense Industrial Base. Multiple strategy documents and directives guide the conduct of military operations in cyberspace, sometimes referred to as cyberwarfare, as well as the delineation of roles and responsibilities for national cybersecurity. Nonetheless, the overarching defense strategy for securing cyberspace is vague and evolving.

This report presents an overview of the threat landscape in cyberspace, including the types of offensive weapons available, the targets they are designed to attack, and the types of actors carrying out the attacks. It presents a picture of what kinds of offensive and defensive tools exist and a brief overview of recent attacks. The report then describes the current status of U.S. capabilities, and the national and international authorities under which the U.S. Department of Defense carries out cyber operations. Of particular interest for policy makers are questions raised by the tension between legal authorities codified at 10 U.S.C., which authorizes U.S. Cyber Command to initiate computer network attacks, and those stated at 50 U.S.C., which enables the National Security Agency to manipulate and extrapolate intelligence data—a tension that Presidential Policy Directive 20 on U.S. Cyber Operations Policy manages by clarifying the Pentagon's rules of engagement for cyberspace. With the task of defending the nation from cyberattack, the lines of command, jurisdiction, and authorities may be blurred as they apply to offensive and defensive cyberspace operations. A closely related issue is whether U.S. Cyber Command should remain a sub-unified command under U.S. Strategic Command that shares assets and its commander with the NSA. Additionally, the unique nature of cyberspace raises new jurisdictional issues as U.S. Cyber Command organizes, trains, and equips its forces to protect the networks that undergird critical infrastructure. International law governing cyberspace operations is evolving, and may have gaps for determining the rules of cyberwarfare, what constitutes an "armed attack" or "use of force" in cyberspace, and what treaty obligations may be invoked.

Chapter 2 – The information and communications technology (ICT) industry has evolved greatly over the last half century. The technology is ubiquitous and increasingly integral to almost every facet of modern society. ICT devices and components are generally interdependent, and disruption of one may affect many others. Over the past several years, experts and policy makers have expressed increasing concerns about protecting ICT systems from cyberattacks, which many experts expect to increase in frequency and severity over the next several years.

The act of protecting ICT systems and their contents has come to be known as cybersecurity. A broad and arguably somewhat fuzzy concept, cybersecurity can be a useful term but tends to defy precise definition. It is also sometimes inappropriately conflated with other concepts such as privacy, information sharing, intelligence gathering, and surveillance. However, cybersecurity can be an important tool in protecting privacy and preventing unauthorized surveillance, and information sharing and intelligence gathering can be useful tools for effecting cybersecurity.

The management of risk to information systems is considered fundamental to effective cybersecurity. The risks associated with any attack depend on three factors: threats (who is attacking), vulnerabilities (how they are attacking), and impacts (what the attack does). Most cyberattacks have limited impacts, but a successful attack on some components of critical infrastructure (CI)—most of which is held by the private sector—could have significant effects on national security, the economy, and the livelihood and safety of individual citizens. Reducing such risks usually involves removing threat sources, addressing vulnerabilities, and lessening impacts.

The federal role in cybersecurity involves both securing federal systems and assisting in protecting nonfederal systems. Under current law, all federal agencies have cybersecurity responsibilities relating to their own systems, and many have sector-specific responsibilities for CI. On average, federal agencies spend more than 10% of their annual ICT budgets on cybersecurity.

More than 50 statutes address various aspects of cybersecurity, and new legislation has been debated since at least the 111th Congress. Executive Order 13636 and Presidential Policy Directive 21, released in February 2013, address the cybersecurity of CI through voluntary public/private sector collaboration and use of existing regulatory authorities. Four bills enacted in December 2014 address the security of federal ICT, the cybersecurity workforce at the Department of Homeland Security (DHS), and DHS information-sharing activities. Other bills would address information sharing more broadly, research and development, protection of CI, notification of victims of data breaches, and cybercrime laws, among other issues.

The executive-branch actions and proposed legislation are largely designed to address several well-established near-term needs in cybersecurity. However, those needs exist in the context of more difficult long-term challenges relating to design, incentives, consensus, and environment. Legislation and executive actions in the 114th Congress could have significant impacts on those challenges.

Chapter 3 – The federal role in cybersecurity has been a topic of discussion and debate for over a decade. Despite significant legislative efforts in the 112th Congress on bills designed to improve the cybersecurity of U.S. critical infrastructure (CI), no legislation on that issue was enacted in that Congress. In an effort to address the issue in the absence of enacted legislation, the White House issued an executive order in February 2013. Citing repeated cyber-intrusions into critical infrastructure and growing cyberthreats, Executive Order 13636, *Improving Critical Infrastructure Cybersecurity,* was an attempt to enhance security and resiliency of CI through voluntary, collaborative efforts involving federal agencies and owners and operators of privately owned CI, as well as use of existing federal regulatory authorities.

Entities posing a significant threat to the cybersecurity of CI assets include cyberterrorists, cyberspies, cyberthieves, cyberwarriors, and cyberhacktivists. E.O. 13636 has attempted to address such threats by, among other things,

- expanding to other CI sectors an existing Department of Homeland Security (DHS) program for information sharing and collaboration between the government and the private sector;
- establishing a broadly consultative process for identifying CI with especially high priority for protection;
- requiring the National Institute of Standards and Technology (NIST) to lead in developing a cybersecurity framework of standards and best practices for protecting CI; and
- directing regulatory agencies to determine the adequacy of existing requirements and their authority to establish additional ones to address the risks.

Among the major issues covered by the unenacted legislative proposals in the 112th Congress, E.O. 13636 mainly addresses two: information sharing and protection of privately held critical infrastructure. It does not provide exemptions from liability stemming from information sharing, which would require changes to current law. Several of the legislative proposals included such changes. With respect to protection of critical infrastructure, the provisions on designation of CI and identification of relevant regulations are related to those in some legislative proposals.

In the 113th Congress, some bills would provide explicit statutory authority for information-sharing along the lines of some bills in the 112th Congress. Others would authorize activities on developing a cybersecurity framework similar to those in the executive order.

The issuance of E.O. 13636, as with many other executive orders, raises questions about whether the order exceeds the scope of the President's authority, in relation to the constitutional separation of powers and validly enacted legislation. While answers to those questions are complex, the executive order specifies that implementation will be consistent with applicable law and that nothing in the order provides regulatory authority to an agency beyond that under existing law.

Overall, response to the executive order has been optimistic. Given the absence of comprehensive cybersecurity legislation, some security observers contend that the order is a necessary step in securing vital assets against cyberthreats. Others have argued, in contrast, that it offers little more than do existing processes, that it could make enactment of a bill less likely, or that it could lead to government intrusiveness into private-sector activities, for example through increased regulation under existing statutory authority. Despite considerable progress in meeting the specific objectives in the executive order, especially the NIST Framework, it still appears to be too early in the implementation of the order to determine whether such concerns will be addressed to the satisfaction of critics and skeptics.

Chapter 4 – The number of cyber incidents reported by federal agencies increased in fiscal year 2013 significantly over the prior 3 years (see figure). An effective response to a cyber incident is essential to minimize any damage that might be caused. DHS and US-CERT have a role in helping agencies detect, report, and respond to cyber incidents.

GAO was asked to review federal agencies' ability to respond to cyber incidents. To do this, GAO reviewed the extent to which (1) federal agencies are effectively responding to cyber incidents and (2) DHS is providing cybersecurity incident assistance to agencies. To do this, GAO used a statistical sample of cyber incidents reported in fiscal year 2012 to project whether 24 major federal agencies demonstrated effective response activities. In addition, GAO evaluated incident response policies, plans, and procedures at 6 randomly-selected federal agencies to determine adherence to federal guidance. GAO also examined DHS and US-CERT policies, procedures, and practices, and surveyed officials from the 24 federal agencies on their experience receiving incident assistance from DHS.

In: Cyberspace Threat Landscape
Editor: Cody L. Barker

ISBN: 978-1-63482-338-8

Chapter 1

CYBER OPERATIONS IN DOD POLICY AND PLANS: ISSUES FOR CONGRESS*

Catherine A. Theohary and Anne I. Harrington

SUMMARY

Cyberspace is defined by the Department of Defense as a global domain consisting of the interdependent networks of information technology infrastructures and resident data, including the Internet, telecommunications networks, computer systems, and embedded processors and controllers. Attacks in cyberspace have seemingly been on the rise in recent years with a variety of participating actors and methods. As the United States has grown more reliant on information technology and networked critical infrastructure components, many questions arise about whether the nation is properly organized to defend its digital strategic assets. Cyberspace integrates the operation of critical infrastructures, as well as commerce, government, and national security. Because cyberspace transcends geographic boundaries, much of it is outside the reach of U.S. control and influence.

The Department of Homeland Security is the lead federal agency responsible for securing the nation's non-security related digital assets. The Department of Defense also plays a role in defense of cyberspace. The National Military Strategy for Cyberspace Operations instructs DOD

* This is an edited, reformatted and augmented version of a Congressional Research Service publication R43848, prepared for Members and Committees of Congress, dated January 5, 2015.

to support the DHS, as the lead federal agency, in national incident response and support to other departments and agencies in critical infrastructure and key resources protection. DOD is responsible for defensive operations on its own information networks as well as the sector-specific agency for the defense of the Defense Industrial Base. Multiple strategy documents and directives guide the conduct of military operations in cyberspace, sometimes referred to as cyberwarfare, as well as the delineation of roles and responsibilities for national cybersecurity. Nonetheless, the overarching defense strategy for securing cyberspace is vague and evolving.

This report presents an overview of the threat landscape in cyberspace, including the types of offensive weapons available, the targets they are designed to attack, and the types of actors carrying out the attacks. It presents a picture of what kinds of offensive and defensive tools exist and a brief overview of recent attacks. The report then describes the current status of U.S. capabilities, and the national and international authorities under which the U.S. Department of Defense carries out cyber operations. Of particular interest for policy makers are questions raised by the tension between legal authorities codified at 10 U.S.C., which authorizes U.S. Cyber Command to initiate computer network attacks, and those stated at 50 U.S.C., which enables the National Security Agency to manipulate and extrapolate intelligence data—a tension that Presidential Policy Directive 20 on U.S. Cyber Operations Policy manages by clarifying the Pentagon's rules of engagement for cyberspace. With the task of defending the nation from cyberattack, the lines of command, jurisdiction, and authorities may be blurred as they apply to offensive and defensive cyberspace operations. A closely related issue is whether U.S. Cyber Command should remain a sub-unified command under U.S. Strategic Command that shares assets and its commander with the NSA. Additionally, the unique nature of cyberspace raises new jurisdictional issues as U.S. Cyber Command organizes, trains, and equips its forces to protect the networks that undergird critical infrastructure. International law governing cyberspace operations is evolving, and may have gaps for determining the rules of cyberwarfare, what constitutes an "armed attack" or "use of force" in cyberspace, and what treaty obligations may be invoked.

INTRODUCTION[1]

Cyberspace has taken on increased strategic importance as states have begun to think of it as yet another domain—similar to land, sea, and air—that must be secured to protect their national interests. Cyberspace is another dimension, with the potential for both cooperation and conflict. The Obama Administration's 2010 National Security Strategy identifies cybersecurity threats "as one of the most serious national security, public safety, and economic challenges."

Cyberattacks are now a common element of international conflict, both on their own and in conjunction with broader military operations. Targets have included government networks, media outlets, banking services, and critical infrastructure. The effects and implications of such attacks may be small or large; cyberattacks have defaced websites, temporarily shut down networks and cut off access to essential information and services, and damaged industrial infrastructure. Despite being relatively common, cyberattacks are difficult to identify at their source and thwart, in particular because politically motivated attacks are often crowd-sourced,[2] and online criminal organizations are easy to join. Suspicions of state-sponsored cyberattacks are often strong but difficult to prove. The relative anonymity under which actors operate in cyberspace affords a degree of plausible deniability.

This report focuses specifically on cyberattacks as an element of warfare, separate and distinct from diplomatic or industrial espionage, financially motivated cybercrime, or state-based intimidation of domestic political activists.[3] However, drawing clean lines between cyberwar, cyberterrorism, cyberespionage, and cybercrime is difficult. State and non-state actors carry out cyberattacks every day. When and under what conditions cyberattacks rise to the level of cyberwar is an open question. Some experts contend that all warfare, including cyberwarfare, by definition includes the destruction of physical objects. According to this point of view, to be an act of cyberwarfare, the attack must originate in cyberspace and result in the destruction of critical infrastructure, military command-and-control capabilities, and/or the injury or death of individuals.[4] On the other hand, some analysts have a more inclusive view of cyberwarfare. These experts would include, in addition to cyberattacks with kinetic effects, the exfiltration or corruption of data, the disruption of services, and/or manipulation of victims through distraction.

As our military becomes increasingly information dependent, potential vulnerabilities in network-centric operations are crystalized. A cyberattack on a military asset may be considered an act of war to which the military will respond under the Law of Armed Conflict. However, there may also be attacks on civilian systems which would warrant a military response.

BACKGROUND

Cyberspace: The Operating Environment

The Internet represents a portion of the global domain of cyberspace; however, there are networks and systems that are not connected to the Internet. Included among these are national strategic assets whose compromise could have serious consequences. In its 2010 Quadrennial Defense Review, the Department of Defense (DOD) identified cyberspace as a global commons or domain, along with air, sea and space. Previous views of cyberspace had focused mainly on the enabling or force multiplier aspects of information technology and networked workfare. Cyberspace is currently defined by the DOD as a global domain within the information environment consisting of the interdependent networks of information technology infrastructures and resident data, including the Internet, telecommunications networks, computer systems, and embedded processors and controllers.[5] It is also described in terms of three layers: (1) a physical network, (2) a logical network, and a (3) cyber-persona:[6]

- The *physical network* is composed of the geographic and physical network components.
- The *logical network* consists of related elements abstracted from the physical network, (e.g., a website that is hosted on servers in multiple locations but accessed through a single URL).
- The *cyber-persona layer* uses the rules of the logical network layer to develop a digital representation of an individual or entity identity.

Because one individual or entity can have multiple cyber personae, and vice versa, attributing responsibility and targeting attacks in cyberspace is challenging. Another challenge lies in insider threats, when an authorized user or users exploits legitimate access to a network for nefarious purposes.

From a military perspective, the *operational environment* is a composite of the conditions, circumstances, and influences that affect the employment of capabilities and bear on the decisions of the commander.[7] The *information environment* is the aggregate of individuals, organizations, and systems that collect, process, disseminate, or act on information, further broken down into the physical, informational, and cognitive dimensions.

Cyberspace operations employ capabilities whose primary purpose is to achieve objectives in or through cyberspace. The following section gives examples of some of the tools through which these objectives may be achieved.

Cyber Weapons

There are several tools through which effects in cyberspace are achieved. Effects can range in severity from disrupting or slowing down access to online goods and services, to degrading and destroying entire network operations. The actors who employ these tools can range from individual hacker groups to nation states and their proxies. The following section describes the most common attack tools, or cyber weapons, that these actors employ.

Malware

Malware is a general term for malicious software. Bots, viruses, and worms are varieties of malware. Bots, as described below, are used to establish communication channels among personal computers, linking them together into botnets that can be controlled remotely. Botnets are one way that other forms of malware, such as viruses and worms, spread. As the names imply, viruses spread by infecting a host. They attach themselves to a program or document. In contrast, worms are stand alone, self-replicating programs.[8]

The first known malware aimed at PCs, a virus, was coded in 1986 by two brothers in Pakistan. They named the virus Brain after their computer shop in Lahore and included their names, addresses, and phone numbers in the code. Calling Brain malware is slightly misleading because the brothers had no ill intentions. They were simply curious to find out how far their creation could travel. Within a year it had traveled around the globe.[9]

Malware that targets the internal networks of particular companies are often spread by infecting "watering-holes," a term for public websites frequented by employees. Another common method is "spearphishing"—sending emails to targeted individuals that contain malicious links. The email appears to be innocuous and sent from a trusted source, but clicking on the link opens a virtual door to outsiders.[10] So-called "air-gapped" networks, computer systems that are not connected to the Internet, are not vulnerable to these types of attacks; however, such networks can be infected by viruses and worms when an external device, such as a thumb drive, is inserted into a networked computer.

Botnets

Robotic networks, commonly known as botnets, are chains of home and business PCs linked together by a script or program. That program (the bot) enables a single operator to command all of the linked machines. Botnets are not necessarily malicious. The computer code botnets use also enables desirable communication across the Internet, such as the chat rooms that were popular in the 1990s. However, programmers have figured out how to exploit vulnerabilities in widely used Microsoft Windows operating platforms to degrade, destroy, and manipulate computer networks—often without the knowledge of the machine's owner or local operator.[11] Because they are automated programs, when released, bots lurk on the Internet and take over computers, turning them into a network of "zombies" that can be operated remotely. The majority of email spam is generated by botnets without the host computer's knowledge.[12] In fact, owners are often not aware that their computers are part of a botnet, the only indication of which is sluggish response time.[13]

Early botnet operators were often skilled coders. In contrast, today an underground industry of skilled botnet providers exists, but operators no longer have to be fluent coders. Starting in 2004, bots got considerably easier to use as the result of new applications that allowed hackers to build bots by pointing and clicking, resulting in a bloom of spam in email inboxes across the globe.[14] In addition to unwanted advertising, botnets can generate denial-of-service (DoS) attacks and spread malware.

Distributed Denial of Service Attacks

Distributed Denial of Service (DDoS) attacks flood their target with requests, consuming the target's bandwidth and/or overloading the capacity of the host server, resulting in service outages. These attacks are "distributed" because effective attacks employ botnets, distributing the source of requests across an entire network of zombie computers. DDoS attacks are unique for three reasons: (1) they exploit vulnerabilities in their target's software or operating system that cannot be easily repaired or "patched;" (2) each individual packet is a legitimate request—only the rate and total volume of packets gives an attack its destructive impact; and (3) the severity of the attack is measured in terms of its duration. Unlike malware, which alters or infects its target, DDoS attacks consist of the same types of packets, a unit of data, that a typical user would send when making a legitimate request. The only difference is in the number and frequency with which the attacker generates requests. The goal of a DDoS attack is to render targeted networks unavailable or nonresponsive, thereby preventing users from accessing information for the duration of the attack.[15]

The pathway of a DDoS attack is known as a *vector*. Today it is common for an attack to have multiple vectors. A DDoS attack carried out by botnets along multiple vectors can interrupt services for days, weeks, or even months. More sophisticated attacks take advantage of vectors that amplify their strength through a process that generates exponential reverberations. The ability to amplify an attack, for instance by tricking a server into responding to a target with an even larger packet than what was originally sent, increases an already substantial asymmetric advantage. Botnet applications not only make DDoS attacks relatively easy to mount, but the redundant and decentralized nature of the Internet makes attribution difficult.[16] In theory, a DDoS attack could temporarily take down the entire web by simultaneously targeting the 13 root servers on which all Internet traffic depends.[17] In practice, this has not yet happened.

Automated Defense Systems

Retaliatory hacking, a response to network breaches that has been used in the private sector, has gained traction within DOD as a means to stage an "active defense." These potentially offensive operations may occur when a systems administrator sees an intrusion and in turn breaches the assumed point of origin, either to retrieve or destroy information. However, such activities are complicated for two reasons: uncertainty in attack attribution and active defense may violate terms enacted in the Computer Fraud and Abuse Act of 1986.[18] This law criminalizes unauthorized breaches and other computer-related activity, including the distribution of malware and use of botnets. Although the military would be involved in a counterattack only during a national security crisis, the government may tacitly encourage companies to engage in retaliatory hacking as the first line of defense for the nation's critical infrastructure. For example, the Defense Advanced Research Projects Agency (DARPA) has launched a Cyber Grand Challenge program to hasten the development of automated security systems capable of responding to and neutralizing cyberattacks as fast as they are launched. Automated defense systems may also be configured to launch a counterattack in the direction of a network breach.

Targets

Attacks on information technology destroy, degrade, and/or exfiltrate data from a host computer. The intended effect of a cyberattack can be related to the attack target. Within the context of cyberwarfare, two areas are attractive targets for a potential adversary: government and military networks, and critical infrastructure and industrial control systems.

Government and Military Networks

Nation states and other entities target government and military networks to exfiltrate data, thereby gaining an intelligence advantage, or to potentially plant a malicious code that could be activated in a time of crisis to disrupt, degrade, or deny operations. In 2008, The Pentagon itself was a target of a massive breach, when an infected thumb drive was inserted into a computer connected to DOD classified networks. The discovery of the malware, named Agent.btz, led to a massive cleanup operation code-named Buckshot Yankee.[19] While the incident appeared to be related to espionage and theft of sensitive information, it is possible that malware could also contain a hidden, more nefarious function, such as the capability to disable communications or spread disinformation.

Critical Infrastructure and Industrial Control Systems

Civilian critical infrastructure comprises networks and services that are considered vital to a nation's operations and are owned and operated by the private sector.[20] Examples of these sectors include energy, transportation, financial services, food supplies, and communications. These sectors may be particularly vulnerable to cyberattack because they rely on open-source software or hardware, third-party utilities, and interconnected networks.

Large-scale industrial control systems (ICS), such as the supervisory control and data acquisition (SCADA) systems that provide real-time information to remote operators, present a unique vulnerability. Disabling an electric power plant by attacking its SCADA system, for instance, will have many follow-on effects. These systems, as they control the operations of a particular platform, are referred to by the Defense Department as "operations technology."

From highly specialized equipment, such as uranium enrichment plants, to mundane heating and air conditioning systems and office photocopiers, the capability to remotely control industrial hardware for maintenance and operations purposes also makes these machines vulnerable to cyberattacks.

Attacks against operations technology (OT) are different than information technology (IT) attacks because OT attacks can produce kinetic effects. Although OT controls primarily mundane infrastructure, these built environments are increasingly networked environments, which adds a complicated layer to training and maintenance.

Actors and Attribution

With low barriers to entry, multiple actors may take part in use of the Internet and networked technology as a means to achieve strategic effects. These actors may represent nation states, politically motivated hacker groups or "hactivists," or terrorist and other criminal organizations. Directly attributing a cyberattack to any one of these groups can be challenging, particularly as they may sometimes operate in concert with each other, though for differing motivations.

Nation States

Cyberwarriors are agents or quasi-agents of nation states who develop capabilities and undertake cyberattacks to support a country's strategic objectives.[21] These entities may or may not be acting on behalf of the government with respect to target selection, attack timing, or type(s) of cyberattack. Moreover, cyberwarriors are often blamed by the host country when the nation that has been attacked levies accusations against that country. Typically, when a foreign government is presented with evidence that a cyberattack is emanating from its country, the nation that has been attacked is told that the perpetrators acted of their own volition, not at the behest of the government.

Politically Motivated Hacktivists

Cyberhactivists are individuals who perform cyberattacks for pleasure, or for philosophical or other nonmonetary reasons. Examples include someone who attacks a technology system as a personal challenge (who might be termed a "classic" hacker), and a "hacktivist," such as a member of the cybergroup Anonymous, who undertakes an attack for political reasons. The activities of these groups can range from simple nuisance-related DoS attacks to disrupting government and private corporation business processes.

Terrorists and Organized Crime

Cyberterrorists are state-sponsored or non-state actors who engage in cyberattacks as a form of warfare. Transnational terrorist organizations, insurgents, and jihadists have used the Internet as a tool for planning attacks, recruiting and radicalizing members, distributing propaganda, and communicating.[22] No unclassified reports have been published regarding a terrorist-initiated cyberattack on U.S. critical infrastructure. However, the essential components of that infrastructure are demonstrably vulnerable to access and even destruction via the Internet. In 2007, a U.S. Department of Energy test at Idaho Labs demonstrated the ability of a cyberattack to shut down parts of the electrical grid. In the test, known as the Aurora Experiment, a cyberattack on a replica of a power plant's generator caused it to self-destruct.

Advanced Persistent Threats

The term "Advanced Persistent Threat" (APT) has been used within the intelligence community to describe nation-state cyberespionage activities. However, organizations that may or may not be state-sponsored may also use APT techniques to gain a competitive military advantage. Characteristics of an APT include a high level of sophistication in the malware's code, along with the targeting of certain networks or servers to glean specific information of value to the attackers or to cause damage to a specific target. Likely targets include government agencies and corporations in critical infrastructure sectors such as financial, defense, information technology, transportation, and health. In 2013, the U.S. security firm Mandiant published a 60-page intelligence report on a Chinese operation, which the firm identified as APT1, that allegedly stole hundreds of terabytes of data from at least 141 organizations across 20 industries worldwide since 2006.[23] Mandiant's analysis concluded that APT1 is likely government-sponsored (believed to be the 2nd Bureau of the People's Liberation Army General Staff Department's 3rd Department) and one of the most persistent of China's cyber threat actors.

Attribution Issues

Analysts trying to determine the origin of a cyberattack are often stymied by the use of botnets. First, computers infected by a botnet may be located in countries around the world, obscuring the country of origin of the botnet's commander, known as the bot herder. Second, the identity of the server controlling the botnet may be obscured by the prevalence of peer-to-peer software[24]. In addition to these concerns, Internet provider (IP) addresses that might otherwise trace the location of a computer that launched an attack can be faked (known as "spoofing"), and even with a valid IP address, it may be virtually impossible to verify who was behind the computer at the time an attack was launched. This uncertainty is also true of a computer that has been infected unbeknownst to the user. At the nation-state level, a certain amount of deniability in terms of cybersecurity and network control is plausible. Given the proliferation of hacker organizations and the cyber weapons at their disposal, states can easily claim a lack of responsibility for rogue cyber actors and attacks that appear to stem from within state borders.

Threat Environment

Cyberattack is a persistent threat. This section describes events that have provoked a political and/or military response from leaders in one or more state. The case studies provided are not exhaustive; excluded are many instances of cyber espionage that could arguably be considered international incidents. Instead, this section focuses primarily on cyberattacks that (1) have had strategic effects, (2) play a tactical role in a larger military operation, (3) carry implications for the ability of a state to carry out future military operations, or (4) threaten public trust in the reliability and security of information on the Internet.

Cyberattack Case Studies

Each of the cyberattacks in this section illustrates a different tactical and/or strategic use of weapons in cyberspace. The events in each of these cases raised questions about acts of terror and/or war in cyberspace and the role of the military.

Estonia: Cyberattack As Siege

Estonia is a Baltic state of approximately 1.3 million people that regained its independence from the Soviet Union in 1991. In 2004, Estonia joined the European Union (EU). Technologically, Estonia distinguished itself as the home of Skype, a widely popular online voice and video communication software. Today, Estonia is one of the most wired nations on earth. Estonians conduct most of their daily business online, even carrying out the basic rights and responsibilities of democratic citizenship, such as voting, through the Internet. As a result, Estonia is particularly vulnerable to cyberattack.[25]

On the morning of April 28, 2007, waves of DDoS attacks besieged websites in Estonia. Over the next two weeks, attackers targeted crucial sectors, shutting down Internet access to hundreds of key government, banking, and media web pages. Estonians were unable to bank online or retrieve cash from ATMs. Attackers also targeted Internet addresses for servers, threatening the telephone network and the credit card verification system. Vital services simply ceased to function, unable to stand back up before the next wave of attack. Where possible, organizations cut off all international traffic, closing the gates against the attack. Unlike previous DoS attacks that hit a single site over the course of days, this attack brought communication and commerce in a sovereign nation to a halt for weeks.[26]

The 2007 cyberattacks appear to have originated in Russia. On April 27, 2007, Estonian officials carried out a controversial plan to relocate a World War II-era statue of a Red Army soldier from a central location in Tallinn, the nation's capital, to a military cemetery in a suburb. Despite ominous warnings from the Russian government that removing the statue honoring the sacrifice of Russian soldiers would prove "disastrous for Estonians," Estonia, after 16 years of independence, decided to move the reminder of Soviet occupation.[27]

What role, if any, the Russian government actually played in the attack is unclear. The Russian government claimed the attack was an online version of an angry mob. Evidence suggests that patriotic hackers played an important role in the attack. The Pro-Putin movement Nashi ("Ours"), which organizes political events for young adults, claimed at least partial responsibility for engaging in cyber activities to counter "anti-Fatherland" forces.[28] Suspicion remains about government involvement, though. Patriotic hacking can provide cover for behind-the-scenes coordination efforts.

The attacks followed instructions posted in Russian language Internet chat rooms on how to generate DoS attacks. The posts included calls for a coordinated attack at the stroke of midnight on May 9, the day Russians celebrate their World War II victory. At exactly midnight in Moscow, 11p.m. in Tallinn, nearly 1 million computers around the globe navigated to Estonian websites. Surging at 4 million packets per second, Internet traffic in Estonia increased 200-fold, squeezing the bandwidth of an entire nation.[29]

Prepared for the surge, the head of the Estonian computer emergency response team enlisted the help of individuals responsible for the health and care of the Internet root server system to follow attacks back to their source and block specific computers from accessing the servers. This strategy mitigated the effects of the attack. Then suddenly the surges in traffic stopped as suddenly as they had started.[30]

Because Estonia is a member of NATO and the European Union, this event exposed how unprepared those organizations may have been to respond to a cyberattack against a member state. Had Estonia invoked NATO's Article V collective security provision, doing so would have raised several thorny questions about what kind of attack triggers those alliance obligations. The fact that the cyberattack was targeted at a member state and prompted an official state response was complicated by the inability to identify the aggressor. Moreover, the attack did no physical damage, and in the end did no permanent damage to Estonia's web-based infrastructure. The damage was measurable only in terms of short-lived commercial losses.[31] This kind of cyberattack is sometimes likened to a weather event. Snow storms, although a temporary crisis, rarely have any lasting effects. How serious a threat the storm presents depends, at least in part, on one's capability to weather the storm.[32] Although Estonian Defense Ministers viewed this event in terms of a national security crisis, other security analysts described it as a "cyber riot" or "costly nuisance," comparing it to an electronic sit-in where traffic to public and commercial sites is slowed or blocked to make a political point.

Georgia: Cyberattack and Invasion

In 2008, Russia invaded Georgia by land and air and blockaded the nation by sea.

Simultaneously, pro-Russian hackers besieged Georgia's Internet, all but locking down communication for the duration of the armed conflict. Although Georgia is not a heavily wired society—at the time experts ranked it 74th out of 234 nations in terms of Internet addresses, behind Nigeria, Bangladesh, Bolivia, and El Salvador[33]—the attacks were a significant event in the development of cyberwar because they synchronized patriotic hacking with government-sponsored military movements.[34]

Like Estonia, Georgia is a former Soviet state; it declared its independence in 1991. Tensions with Russia have persisted and were not eased by Georgia's failed bid to join NATO in the spring of 2008.[35] Over the course of that same summer, well-armed Russian-backed separatists began consolidating control over two predominately Russian-speaking regions on the country's northern border, Abkhazia and South Ossetia. As tensions rose, separatists—some of whom were believed to be Russian special forces—clashed with Georgian police.[36]

In mid-July, the cyberattacks started. The Georgian President's website was the first high-profile target. Although the DDoS attack vector passed through a U.S.-based, commercial IP address, experts identified the malware that hackers used to generate the attack as a "MachBot" DDoS controller. Machbot is written in Russian and a known tool of Russian criminal groups.[37] Reportedly, pro-Russian hackers were discussing the attacks on websites and in chat rooms; in addition to the higher-profile attack, hackers also temporarily shut down Georgian servers.[38]

Three weeks later, on August 8, Russian tanks crossed the border into South Ossetia. Accompanying the ground invasion was a second round of DDoS attacks. One of the first targets was an online forum popular with pro-Georgian hackers. This preemptive attack reduced, but did not entirely eliminate, the number of counterattacks against Russian targets.[39] As the troops moved in, Georgians were unable to access 54 local websites with critical information related to communications, finance, and the government.[40]

Georgian officials transferred critical Internet resources to U.S., Estonian, and Polish host servers. Refuge for some websites, including those of the President and Ministry of Defense, was granted by an American executive from the privately owned web-hosting company Tulip Systems, but without the knowledge or authority of the U.S. government. Tulip Systems reported experiencing attacks on its servers, a fact that raises troubling questions about sovereignty in the age of cyberwarfare.[41]

The fighting lasted five days. During that time, Georgia's Internet connection was besieged by attacks and unable to communicate via web with the media. Reportedly, cyberattacks followed the same target patterns as the land and air invasions, with DDoS attacks taking out the communications prior to bombing or ground troop movements. Perhaps most importantly, the cyberattacks and the air attack spared critical infrastructure associated with Georgia's energy sector.[42]

Iran: Cyberattack with Kinetic Effect

When programmers at a small Belarussian cybersecurity firm first discovered a new computer worm in June 2010, they knew it was unusually sophisticated because it was exploiting a "zero-day vulnerability" in Microsoft Windows. Malware that outsmarts programmers and developers by identifying an unanticipated weakness in the Windows operating systems is rare. Even so, the cybersecurity specialists who originally detected Stuxnet had no idea just how sophisticated this new worm would turn out to be.[43] The idea of sabotaging industrial control systems from a remote location was not new, but creating a worm that could search for a single target was revolutionary, and this is what Stuxnet's authors had achieved. [44]

The intended target appears to have been industrial control systems in Iran's nuclear facility at Natanz. The first clue was the pattern of infected computers: the Stuxnet worm attacked air-gapped networks (i.e., those not connected to the Internet). The worm propagated by infecting local hosts via a USB thumb drive. While a computer scanned the contents of the inserted thumb drive, the worm surreptitiously installed a partially encrypted file. This file contained a stolen security certificate that fooled its host into believing that the Stuxnet worm was a trusted program. From its initial host computer, Stuxnet could travel throughout a networked system. Although Stuxnet did not propagate itself through the web, if an infected computer was connected to the Internet, the worm would automatically begin sending information back to one of two domain names hosted on servers in Denmark and Malaysia. Once cybersecurity experts realized that infected computers were "phoning home," they redirected that traffic into a sinkhole they controlled. By analyzing the collected data, the experts were able to map the pattern of infection. Unlike most malware, which spreads rapidly through densely networked countries like the United States and South Korea, Stuxnet was overwhelmingly concentrated in Iran. Of the first 38,000 infected computers, 22,000 were located in Iran.[45]

The second clue as to Stuxnet's intended target was that, reportedly starting in 2009, International Atomic Energy Agency inspectors noticed the significantly higher-than-average rate at which Iran was removing and repairing centrifuges in its uranium enrichment facility at Natanz.[46] Centrifuges built to process natural uranium into a form capable of fueling a nuclear power plant, or building a nuclear warhead, are extremely delicate. Among the fastest spinning objects on earth, any irregularities in a centrifuge's rotor will cause imbalances. Even a fingerprint on the rotor would cause it to spin out of control and do irreparable damage.[47] As cybersecurity specialists dug deeper into the code, they identified commands that were specific to the industrial control system Simatic WinCC Step7, produced by the German company Siemens. This is the same controller Iran uses in its uranium-enrichment facilities to control its centrifuges. Once Stuxnet identified its target, the malware automatically commanded the centrifuges to spin at frequencies significantly faster and then slower than normal, doing damage to the delicate rotors. Meanwhile, Stuxnet evaded detection by making it appear to the operators monitoring the system (via a computer screen) that nothing had changed.[48]

The overall effect of Stuxnet on the Iranian nuclear program is unclear. Iran has since acknowledged the attack but maintains that Stuxnet did not change the rate at which it was able to increase its stockpile of enriched uranium.[49] David Albright and Christina Walrond of the Institute for Science and International Security argue that although the rate of production has not changed, starting in late 2009, Iran required more centrifuges to perform the same amount of work. Albright and Walrond did not definitively argue that Stuxnet caused Iran's efficiency to decline, nor did they discount that possibility, instead stating, "It is likely that multiple factors have played a role in the diminished effectiveness of the FEP [fuel enrichment plant].... The available data are too general to determine the actual situation."[50]

No one has claimed responsibility for the attack, but in January 2011, but the *New York Times* reported that Stuxnet was a joint venture of the United States and Israel. Reportedly, Israel constructed a centrifuge plant at Dimona identical to the one in Natanz to simulate the attack. The United States allegedly provided information about vulnerabilities in the Siemens controller, access to which had been gained through a cybersecurity collaboration between Siemens and the Idaho National Lab.[51]

THE DOD AND U.S. CYBER COMMAND

The Department of Defense is responsible for securing its own networks, the Department of Defense information networks (DODIN), or .mil domain, formerly known as the Global Information Grid (GIG). The requested cybersecurity budget for DOD was approximately $5.1 billion for FY2015.This figure represents a portion of the President's requested overall IT budget for DOD that same year (approximately $36 billion). The DOD cybersecurity budget grew by $1 billion from 2013 to 2014, but this increase may reflect changes in how DOD programmatic elements have defined "cybersecurity" programs. In general, the DOD cybersecurity budget comprises the following activities: Information Assurance, Cyberspace Operations, National Cybersecurity Initiative/Defense Industrial Base/Defense Cyber Crime Center, and U.S. Cyber Command.[52]

After recognizing that cyberspace is a global operating domain as well as a strategic national asset, DOD reorganized its cyber resources and established the U.S. Cyber Command in 2010. This sub-unified command under the U.S. Strategic Command is co-located at Fort Meade, Maryland with the National Security Agency (NSA). It combines offensive and defensive capabilities and is commanded by a four-star general, also the director of the NSA. The NSA's primary missions are information assurance for National Security Systems and signals intelligence. Also located within NSA is the Central Security Service, the military's cryptology component. As an intelligence agency, NSA operates under the authorities of Title 50 U.S.C., War and National Defense. U.S. Cyber Command operates under U.S.C. Title 10, Armed Forces—the authorities through which the military organizes, trains, and equips its forces in defense of the nation.

Cyber Command Mission and Force Structure

As previously stated, one of the main missions of U.S Cyber Command is to defend and operate the DODIN. In his nomination hearing before the Senate Armed Services Committee, then-Vice Admiral Michael S. Rogers, tapped to become the head of U.S. Cyber Command, described the duties of the Cyber Commander thusly:

> The Commander, U. S. Cyber Command (USCYBERCOM) is responsible for executing the cyberspace missions specified in Section 18.d.(3)of the Unified Command Plan (UCP) as delegated by the Commander, U.S. Strategic Command (USSTRATCOM) to secure our nation's freedom of action in cyberspace and to help mitigate risks to our national security resulting from America's growing dependence on cyberspace. Subject to such delegation and in coordination with mission partners, specific missions include: directing DODIN operations, securing and defending the DODIN; maintaining freedom of maneuver in cyberspace; executing full-spectrum military cyberspace operations; providing shared situational awareness of cyberspace operations, including indications and warning; integrating and synchronizing of cyberspace operations with combatant commands and other appropriate U.S. Government agencies tasked with defending the our nation's interests in cyberspace; provide support to civil authorities and international partners. All these efforts support DoD's overall missions in cyberspace of defending the nation against cyber attacks, supporting the combatant commands, and defending Department of Defense networks.[53]

Operators at the U.S. Cyber Command are sometimes referred to as "cyber warriors," although this term does not appear in official Department of Defense definitions. Reports of USCYBERCOM-planned workforce structures yield clues regarding the activities a so-called cyber warrior might undertake. First reported in the *Washington Post*, "The plan calls for the creation of three types of Cyber Mission Forces under the Cyber Command: 'national mission forces' to protect computer systems that undergird electrical grids, power plants and other infrastructure deemed critical to national and economic security; 'combat mission forces' to help commanders abroad plan and execute attacks or other offensive operations; and 'cyber protection forces' to fortify the Defense Department's networks."[54]

These multiservice Cyber Mission Forces numbered under 1,000 in 2013, when DOD announced plans to expand them to roughly 5,000 soldiers and civilians. The target number has since grown to 6,200, with a deadline at the end of FY2016. In early November 2014, a leaked classified document was reported to have stated that "additional capability may be needed for both surge capacity for the [Cyber Mission Forces] and to provide unique and specialized capabilities" for a whole-of-government and nation approach to security in cyberspace.[55] USCYBERCOM Commander Admiral Michael S. Rogers has said that overall, Cyber Mission Forces will be about 80% military and 20% civilian. At a recent conference, Deputy Commander of USCYBERCOM Lieutenant General James McLaughlin said the Cyber Mission Force was being formed into 133 teams of tactical units that will [56]support all Combatant Commands, and that at least half of these teams would be used for defensive measures.

Each of the four military services provides cyber mission forces to USCYBERCOM. All of the services' cyber divisions plan to steadily increase their number of cyber operators over the next two years.

USCYBERCOM and Information Sharing

In May 2011, DOD launched a pilot voluntary program (the DIB Cyber Pilot) involving several defense industry partners, the NSA and DOD, to share classified threat-vector information among stakeholders. Under the DIB Cyber Pilot, NSA shares threat signatures with participating defense companies. One aspect of the program was sharing by the NSA of threat signatures obtained through its computer monitoring activities. DHS subsequently initiated the Joint Cybersecurity Services Pilot (JCSP) in January 2012 and announced in July that the program would be made permanent, with the renamed DIB Enhanced Cybersecurity Services (DECS) as the first phase. In this program, DHS communicates with participating commercial Internet service providers directly, while DOD still serves as the point of contact for participating DIB contractors.

AUTHORITIES

Authorities for U.S. military operations in cyberspace are not currently organized according to the nature of the perceived threat, whether espionage, crime, or war. Instead, authorities are organized according to the domain (.mil, .gov, .com, etc.) in which the activity is taking place, as opposed to its motivations or effects. Presidential Policy Directive 20, discussed in greater detail below, distinguishes between *network defense* on the one hand and *offensive and defensive cyberspace operations* on the other.

U.S. policy on network defense is to adopt a risk-management framework published by the Department of Commerce's National Institute of Standards and Technology. Responsibility for implementing the framework is shared among different government departments and agencies, with U.S. Cyber Command responsible for the .mil domain and the Department of Homeland Security responsible for the .gov domain. Adoption of the NIST framework is voluntary for private companies and their own network defense.

One of the instruments through which offensive cyberspace operations are conducted may be a classified "Execute Order," defined by DOD as an order issued by the Chairman of the Joint Chiefs of Staff, at the direction of the Secretary of Defense, to implement a decision by the President to initiate military operations.[57] According to The Federation of American Scientists' *Secrecy News,* Air Force Instruction 10-1701, entitled "Command and Control (C2) for Cyberspace Operations," dated March 5, 2014, states, "Classified processes governing C2 [command and control] of AF [Air Force] offensive and defensive cyberspace operations conducted by AF Cyber Mission Forces are addressed in a classified CJCS [Chairman, Joint Chiefs of Staff] Execute Order (title classified) issued on 21 Jun 13."[58] Then-Vice Admiral Michael Rogers, as a nominee for Commander, U.S. Cyber Command (and NSA Director), said before the Senate Armed Services Committee that "geographic combatant commanders already have authority to direct and execute certain Defensive Cyberspace Operations (DCO) within their own networks." However, the Execute Order suggests that there may be standing orders to conduct offensive cyberspace operations as well.

The following section provides a brief overview of evolving norms in cyberspace and the authorities that govern network defense and cyberspace operations.

Legislative Authorities

Section 941of the National Defense Authorization Act for Fiscal Year 2013 (P.L. 112-239), affirms the Secretary of Defense's authority to conduct military activities in cyberspace. The provision's language is similar to that in Section 954 of final conference report to accompany H.R. 1540, the National Defense Authorization Act for Fiscal Year 2012. In this version, this section reaffirms that the Secretary of Defense has the authority to conduct military activities in cyberspace. In particular, it clarifies that the Secretary of Defense has the authority to conduct clandestine cyberspace activities in support of military operations pursuant to a congressionally authorized use of force outside of the United States, or to defend against a cyberattack on an asset of the DOD.[59] The section highlights the blurred lines between military operations and intelligence activities, particularly with respect to cyberspace. In general, Title 10 and Title 50 of the U.S. Code refer to distinct chains of command and missions belonging to the armed forces and intelligence agencies, respectively. The U.S. Cyber Command, the military entity responsible for offensive operations in cyberspace and subject to Title 10 authorities, is co-located with and led by the Director of the National Security Agency, a Title 50 intelligence organization. Computer Network Attack, the military parlance for offensive operations, is closely related to and at times indistinguishable from Computer Network Exploitation, which is used to denote data extrapolation or manipulation.

According to DOD, a clandestine operation is one that is "sponsored or conducted by governmental departments or agencies in such a way as to assure secrecy or concealment. A clandestine operation differs from a covert operation in that emphasis is placed on concealment of the operation rather than on concealment of the identity of the sponsor."[60] Under Title 50, a "covert action" is subject to presidential finding and Intelligence Committee notification requirements. Traditional military activity, although undefined, is an explicit exception to the Title 50 U.S.C. covert action definition in Section 913 as the identity of the sponsor of a traditional military activity may be well known.

According to the Joint Explanatory Statement of the Committee of Conference, H.R. 1455, July 25, 1991, traditional military activities

> include activities by military personnel under the direction and control of a United States military commander (whether or not the U.S. sponsorship of such activities is apparent or later to be acknowledged)

preceding and related to hostilities which are either anticipated (meaning approval has been given by the National Command Authorities for the activities and or operational planning for hostilities) to involve U.S. military forces, or where such hostilities involving United States military forces are ongoing, and, where the fact of the U.S. role in the overall operation is apparent or to be acknowledged publicly.

By this reading, a clandestine operation falls under the traditional military activity rubric, because the identity of the sponsor is not concealed. Hence, by referring only to "clandestine" operations rather than covert operations, the provision distinguishes between approval and reporting requirements for military-directed cyberspace operations and those conducted by the intelligence community. By requiring quarterly briefings to the congressional defense committees, the language would also appear to address concerns that a "clandestine" or "traditional military activity" designation for a cyber operation would skirt the strict oversight requirements of its covert counterpart. However, confusion may remain regarding the proper role and requirements of the military, because some cyber operations may contain both covert and clandestine elements. Another consideration is the military's responsibility to notify congressional intelligence committees of computer network exploitation activities undertaken as "operational preparation of the environment."

Executive Authorities

In December 2008, President-elect Obama offered details about the cybersecurity goals his Administration would pursue, including "strengthening federal leadership on cybersecurity, developing next-generation secure computers and networking for national security applications, and protecting the IT infrastructure to prevent corporate cyberespionage."[61] In February 2009, he initiated a 60-day interagency review with the goal of developing "a strategic framework to ensure" that federal cybersecurity initiatives "are appropriately integrated, resourced, and coordinated with Congress and the private sector."[62] The White House released the *Cyberspace Policy Review* in May 2009.[63] At that time, the President announced[64] that the Administration would "pursue a new comprehensive approach to securing America's digital infrastructure," and that he was creating a new White House office to be led by a Cybersecurity Coordinator—a senior cybersecurity policy official, often referred to as the "Cyber Czar," assigned to the Office of the President and responsible for coordinating the nation's cybersecurity-related policies.

While many security observers saw these initial efforts by the Obama Administration as a positive step, others were concerned that government-wide collaborative efforts were not keeping pace with the threats directed at U.S. technological global interests. Between 2009 and 2013, cyber threats to U.S. infrastructure and other assets became a growing concern to policy makers.[65]

In the absence of legislative action, in 2012 the Obama Administration announced a new Presidential policy directive related to U.S. Cyber Operations, the contents of which remain classified, and began drafting an executive order on cybersecurity practices, Executive Order 13636, Improving Critical Infrastructure Cybersecurity, released after a year of interagency debate and review.

At the federal level, five executive orders and Presidential directives authorize offensive and defensive action in cyberspace.

National Security Presidential Directive 54/Homeland Security Presidential Directive 23—The Comprehensive National Cybersecurity Initiative

The Obama Administration's *Cyberspace Policy Review* builds on the Comprehensive National Cybersecurity Initiative (CNCI) launched in January 2008 by the George W. Bush Administration via a classified presidential directive.[66] The CNCI established a multipronged approach for the federal government to identify threats, address telecommunications and information-system vulnerabilities, and respond to or proactively address entities that wish to steal or manipulate protected data on secure federal systems.[67]

Presidential Policy Directive 20 (PPD-20)—U.S. Cyber Operations Policy

President Obama implemented PPD-20 on U.S. Cyber Operations Policy in October 2012. Although subsequently leaked to the public in June of 2013,[68] PPD-20's contents remain classified, with the exception of what the White House shared in a brief fact sheet. A widely cited *Washington Post* article published on November 14, 2012 asserted the significance of PPD-20:

> For the first time ... the directive explicitly makes a distinction between network defense and cyber-operations to guide officials charged with making often-rapid decisions when confronted with threats. The policy also lays out a process to vet any operations outside government

and defense networks and ensure that U.S. citizens' and foreign allies' data and privacy are protected and international laws of war are followed.

The article went on to quote an unnamed senior administration official on the distinction between defense and offense, clarifying that "network defense is what you're doing inside your own networks.... Cyber-operations is stuff outside that space, and recognizing that you could be doing that for what might be called defensive purposes." [69]

PPD-20 closes a perceived gap in the authorities necessary for DOD to defend the nation in cyberspace, a gap that has not been addressed by Congress. The directive does not create new powers for federal agencies or the military; however, by distinguishing between network defense and cyber operations, it provides a policy framework for the Pentagon's rules of engagement for cyberspace. As specifically described in the White House fact sheet, PPD-20:

- takes into account the evolution of the threat and growing experience with the threat;
- establishes principles and processes for using cyber operations so cyber tools are integrated with the full array of national security tools;
- provides a whole-of-government approach consistent with values promoted domestically and internationally and articulated in the International Strategy for Cyberspace;
- mandates that the United States take the least action necessary to mitigate threats; and
- prioritizes network defense and law enforcement as preferred courses of action.[70]

Executive Order 13636—Improving Critical Infrastructure Cybersecurity

The White House released EO 13636 on February 12, 2013. This executive order declares that "it is the policy of the United States to enhance the security and resilience of the Nation's critical infrastructure (CI) and to maintain a cyber environment that encourages efficiency, innovation, and economic prosperity while promoting safety, security, business confidentiality, privacy, and civil liberties" (Section 1). The order:

- expands information sharing and collaboration between the government and the private sector, including sharing classified information by broadening a program developed for the defense industrial base to other CI sectors;

- develops a voluntary framework of cybersecurity standards and best practices for CI protection, through a public/private effort;
- establishes a consultative process for improving CI cybersecurity;
- identifies CI with especially high priority for protection, using the consultative process;
- establishes a program with incentives for voluntary adoption of the framework by CI owners and operators;
- reviews cybersecurity regulatory requirements to determine whether they are sufficient and appropriate; and
- incorporates privacy and civil liberties protections in activities under the order.

In addition to codifying the DECS program, the order provides specific responsibilities to DHS and the sector-specific agencies, as well as the Departments of Commerce, Defense, and Justice, the intelligence community, the General Services Administration, and the Office of Management and Budget, addressed below.

Presidential Policy Directive 21—Critical Infrastructure Security and Resilience

Along with EO 13636, the White House released Presidential Policy Directive 21 (PPD-21),[71] "Critical Infrastructure Security and Resilience," which addresses the protection of CI. PPD-21 supersedes Homeland Security Presidential Directive 7 (HSPD 7), "Critical Infrastructure Identification, Prioritization, and Protection," released December 17, 2003. PPD-21 seeks to strengthen the security and resilience of CI by

- clarifying functional relationships among federal agencies, including the establishment of separate DHS operational centers for physical and cyberinfrastructure;
- identifying baseline requirements for information sharing;
- applying integration and analysis capabilities in DHS to prioritize and manage risks and impacts, recommend preventive and responsive actions, and support incident management and restoration efforts for CI; and

- organizing research and development (R&D) to enable secure and resilient CI, enhance impact-modeling capabilities, and support strategic DHS guidance.

The directive provides specific responsibilities to DHS and the sector-specific agencies, as well as the Departments of Commerce, Interior, Justice, and State; the intelligence community; the General Services Administration; and the Federal Communications Commission.

National Infrastructure Protection Plan, National Response Framework and Defense Support for Civil Authorities

The National Infrastructure Response Plan (NIPP), developed by DHS with other federal agencies and private sector owners of critical infrastructure, outlines how government and private sector critical infrastructure stakeholders work together to manage risks and achieve security and resiliency. The NIPP 2013 meets the requirements of PPD-21, "Critical Infrastructure and Resilience."

The phrase "defense support of civil authorities" refers to DOD's mission to help civil authorities respond to a domestic emergency or other domestic activity. This support may be provided through the military services, the National Guard, and other DOD resources. For the civil cybersecurity mission, DHS leads the interagency with DOD support. The National Cyber Incident Response Plan outlines roles and responsibilities for coordinating and executing a response to a domestic cyber incident.[72] This plan fits into DHS's National Response Framework, a tiered response guide for local, state, and federal governments with respect to major disasters or emergencies. A 2010 memorandum of agreement between DOD and DHS also guides cooperation between the two entities with respect to securing national cyber assets.[73]

International Authorities

The DOD's role in defense of cyberspace follows the body of laws, strategies, and directives outlined above. For the military to respond to an act of cyberterrorism or cyberwar, a presidential finding must be issued and an order must be executed. However, discussions have been underway in various international fora that may affect how the U.S. government views certain actions in cyberspace and when a military response is warranted. Although the President still decides ultimately what the military will do, the decisions made in the international arena could affect how the Department of Defense organizes, trains, and equips its forces in order to fulfill treaty obligations.

As of yet, no international instruments have been drafted explicitly to regulate inter-state relations in cyberspace. One apparent reason for the absence of such a treaty is that the international governance of cyberspace has largely been the purview of private, professional organizations such as the Internet Engineering Task Force (IETF) and the Internet Corporation for Assigned Names and Numbers (ICANN). However, politically motivated cyberattacks are increasingly common and, although difficult to attribute, often raise strong suspicion of government involvement. More importantly, perhaps, states have become targets of cyberattack, provoking a sense of urgency regarding the creation of national strategies and capabilities for cyberdefense and cyberoffense.

The U.S. Position on International Authorities

The Obama Administration has responded to the internationalization of the cyberspace threat environment by releasing in 2011 an *International Strategy for Cyberspace*.[74] The Strategy calls for strengthening bilateral and multilateral government partnerships, and a strong role for the private sector. It does not call for any new treaties or agreements, and the only existing instrument cited is the Budapest Convention (discussed below). It recommends, instead, preservation of the openness that has been a hallmark of the Internet age. This puts the United States at odds with China and Russia, both of which prefer a more nationalistic approach to Internet governance.

In September 2012, the U.S. State Department, for the first time, took a public position on whether cyber activities could constitute a use of force under Article 2(4) of the U.N. Charter and customary international law. According to State's then-legal advisor, Harold Koh, "Cyber activities that proximately result in death, injury, or significant destruction would likely be viewed as a use of force."[75] Examples offered in Koh's remarks included triggering a meltdown at a nuclear plant, opening a dam and causing flood damage, and causing airplanes to crash by interfering with air traffic control. By focusing on the ends achieved rather than the means with which they are carried out, this definition of cyberwar fits easily within existing international legal frameworks. If an actor employs a cyber weapon to produce kinetic effects that might warrant fire power under other circumstances, then the use of that cyber weapon rises to the level of the use of force.

However, the United States recognizes that cyberattacks without kinetic effects are also an element of armed conflict under certain circumstances.

Koh explained that cyberattacks on information networks in the course of an ongoing armed conflict would be governed by the same principles of proportionality that apply to other actions under the law of armed conflict. These principles include retaliation in response to a cyberattack with a proportional use of kinetic force. In addition, "computer network activities that amount to an armed attack or imminent threat thereof" may trigger a nation's right to self-defense under Article 51 of the U.N. Charter. Here Koh cites the *International Strategy for Cyberspace*, which affirmed that "when warranted, the United States will respond to hostile acts in cyberspace as we would to any other threat to our country." The International Strategy goes on to say that the U.S. reserves the right to use all means necessary – diplomatic, informational, military, and economic – as appropriate and consistent with applicable law, and exhausting all options before military force whenever possible.

International Consensus-Building Activities

One of the Defense Objectives of the *International Strategy for Cyberspace* is to work internationally "to encourage responsible behavior and oppose those who would seek to disrupt networks and systems, dissuading and deterring malicious actors, and reserving the right to defend national assets." A growing awareness of the threat environment in cyberspace has led to two major international processes geared toward developing international expert consensus international cyber authorities.

First, the threat environment has spurred NATO interest in understanding how existing international law applies to cyberwarfare. A year after the 2007 DDoS attack on Estonia, NATO established the Cooperative Cyber Defense Center of Excellence (CCDCOE) in Tallinn, Estonia. The CCDCOE hosts workshops and courses on law and ethics in cyberspace, as well as cyber-defense exercises. In 2009, the center convened an international group of independent experts to draft a manual on the law governing cyberwarfare. The Tallinn Manual, as it is known, was published in 2013. It sets out 95 "black letter rules" governing cyber conflict addressing sovereignty, state responsibility, the law of armed conflict, humanitarian law, and the law of neutrality. The Tallinn Manual is an academic text: although it offers reasonable justifications for the application of international law, it is non-binding and the authors stress that they do not speak for NATO or the CCDCOE.

Second, the cyberspace threat environment has prompted the United Nations to convene Groups of Governmental Experts (GGE) to study

"Developments in the Field of Information and Telecommunications in the Context of International Security." The first successful U.N. GGE report came out in 2010, followed by a second report in 2013. The current GGE is expected to reach consensus again in 2015. The stated purpose of this process is to build "cooperation for a peaceful, secure, resilient and open ICT environment" by agreeing upon "norms, rules and principles of responsible behaviour by States" and identifying confidence and capacity-building measures, including for the exchange of information. Unlike the work done at Tallinn under the auspices of NATO, this U.S.-led process includes both China and Russia.

Existing International Instruments That Bear on Cyberwarfare

As previously discussed, the military's role in cyberwarfare is governed by U.S. law. Yet many international instruments bear on cyberwarfare, including those relating to law enforcement (e.g., extradition and mutual legal assistance treaties), defense, and security, along with broad treaties and agreements, such as the United Nations Charter and the Geneva Conventions, as well as international law. Such instruments include, but are not limited to, those described below.

Council of Europe Convention on Cybercrime

This law-enforcement treaty, also known as the Budapest Convention, requires signatories to adopt criminal laws against specified types of activities in cyberspace, to empower law-enforcement agencies to investigate such activities, and to cooperate with other signatories. Those activities include both attacks on the integrity of cyber-systems and content-related crimes such as fraud, pornography, and "hate speech." The convention focuses on identification and punishment of criminals rather than prevention of cybercrime. Consequently, it may act as a deterrent, but it has no remediating effect on the criminal acts that do occur. Also, the provisions on content may not be consistent with the different approaches of various nations to freedom of expression. While widely cited as the most substantive international agreement relating to cybersecurity, some observers regard it as unsuccessful.[76]

In addition to most members of the Council of Europe, the United States and three other nations have ratified the treaty.[77]

United Nations Resolutions

A series of U.N. General Assembly resolutions relating to cybersecurity have been adopted over the past 15 years. One resolution called for a report from an international group of government experts from 15 nations, including the United States. That 2010 report, sometimes referred to as the Group of Governmental Experts (GGE) Report, recommended a series of steps to "reduce the risk of misperception resulting from ICT[78] disruptions" but did not incorporate any binding agreements.[79] Nevertheless, some observers believe the report represents progress in overcoming differences between the United States and Russia about various aspects of cybersecurity.[80] In December 2001, the General Assembly approved Resolution 56/183, which endorsed the World Summit on the Information Society (WSIS) to discuss on information society opportunities and challenges. This summit was first convened in Geneva, in 2003, and then in Tunis, in 2005, and a1 0-year follow-on in Geneva in May 2013. Delegates from 175 countries took part in the first summit, where they adopted a Declaration of Principles—a road map for achieving an open information society. The Geneva summit left other, more controversial issues unresolved, including the question of Internet governance and funding. At both summits, proposals for the United States to relinquish control of ICANN were rejected.

Law of War

The so-called "Law of War" embodied in the Geneva and Hague Conventions and the U.N. Charter may in some circumstances apply to cyberattacks, but without attempts by nation states to apply it, or specific agreement on its applicability, its relevance remains unclear. It is also complicated by difficulties in attribution, the potential use of botnets (see the "Malware" section above), and possible harm to third parties from cyber-counterattacks, which may be difficult to contain. In addition, questions of territorial boundaries and what constitutes an armed attack in cyberspace remain. The law's application would appear clearest in situations where a cyberattack causes physical damage, such as disruption of an electric grid. As mentioned above, the Tallinn Manual addresses many of these questions.[81]

International Law on Countermeasures

This body of international law relates to "how states may respond to international law violations that do not rise to the level of an armed attack justifying self-defense." It does not expressly address cyberattacks but presumably would be applicable to them, provided the countermeasures target the responsible nation and are "temporary and instrumentally directed" to induce cessation of the violation.[82] Similar caveats apply to such countermeasures with respect to attribution and effects on innocent parties.

North Atlantic Treaty Organization (NATO)

Since the 2007 attack on Estonia,[83] NATO has established authorities relating to cyberdefense, with the goals of advancing strategy and centralizing defense capabilities across members. A policy on cyberdefense[84] and an associated action plan were adopted in 2011, and the NATO Communications and Information Agency (NCIA) was established in 2012 to facilitate the centralization effort.[85] The NATO Cyber Center of Excellence located in Tallinn, Estonia, is another source of legal analysis.

International Telecommunications Regulations

The International Telecommunication Union (ITU) regulates international telecommunications through binding treaties and regulations and nonbinding standards. Regulations prohibit interference with other nations' communication services and permit control of non-state telecommunications for security purposes. The regulations do not, however, expressly forbid military cyberattacks. Also, ITU apparently has little enforcement authority.[86]

Other International Law

Some bodies of international law, especially those relating to aviation and the sea, may be applicable to cybersecurity; for example by prohibiting the disruption of air traffic control or other conduct that might jeopardize aviation safety.[87] Bilaterally, mutual legal assistance treaties between countries may be applicable for cybersecurity forensic investigations and prosecution.

Defense Instruments

The United States has signed 16 treaties and other agreements with 13 other countries and the European Union that include information security, mostly of classified military information, or defense-related information assurance and protection of computer networks. According to news reports, the United States and Australia have agreed to include cybersecurity cooperation within a defense treaty, declaring that a cyberattack on one country would result in retaliation by both.[88]

Other International Organizations

A number of regional associations of nation states have issued declarations of goals and statements of intent relating to cybersecurity, including:

- the G8 Group of States,
- the Asian Pacific Economic Cooperation (APEC),
- the Organization of American States (OAS),
- the Association of South East Asian Nations (ASEAN),
- the Arab League, and
- the Organization for Economic Cooperation and Development (OECD).

However, none of the documents issued by these organizations appear to be binding in effect.[89]

SCO-Proposed International Code of Conduct for Information Security

In September 2011, members of the Shanghai Cooperation Organization, including Russia and China, submitted a proposed voluntary code of conduct for cybersecurity and requested that it be placed on the U.N. General Assembly agenda.[90] Its focus on the rights of governments, such as "reaffirming that policy authority for Internet-related public issues is the sovereign right of States," among other concerns, led to resistance from the United States and other countries.[91]

OSCE Early Warning Resolution

Under the auspices of the Organization for Security and Cooperation in Europe (OSCE), in 2011 and 2012, the United States, Russia, and other countries negotiated a possible agreement that would warn parties early on when cyber-operations might lead to unintentional conflict, but they were unable to reach consensus on the resolution.[92] Although some observers have expressed interest in such an agreement, others doubt its effectiveness, arguing that conflicting interests and the difficulties of attribution, among other problems, make it unfeasible.[93]

ITU Dubai Summit

The ITU convened the World Conference on International Telecommunications (WCIT) in Dubai, United Arab Emirates, during December 3-14, 2012, to review the International Telecommunications Regulations. In the run-up to the summit, many security observers expressed concern over the closed nature of the talks and feared a shift of Internet control away from private entities such as ICANN toward the U.N. and national governments. Although these concerns proved to be largely baseless, a controversial deep packet inspection proposal from the People's Republic of China was adopted at the summit.[94] Dissenting countries, including Germany, fear that this recommendation will result in accelerated Internet censorship in repressed nations.

ISSUES FOR CONGRESS

Authorities: Is Current Law Enough?

Does the military have the authorities it needs to effectively fight and win wars in cyberspace? Some have argued that to fulfill its homeland defense mission, USCYBERCOM should be given increased authority over private sector critical infrastructure protection. Yet business owners, particularly in the IT sector, contend that this would represent a "militarization of cyberspace" that would create distrust among consumers and shareholders, and could potentially stifle innovation, leading to decreases in profits. Others argue that the military's role is to fight and win wars, rather than to bolster a private company's cyber defenses.

As discussed, the international community must contend with a certain amount of ambiguity regarding what constitutes an "armed attack" attack in cyberspace and what the thresholds are for cyberattack as an act of war, an incident of national significance, or both. Without clear redlines and specific consequences articulated, deterrence strategies may be incomplete. On the other hand, a lack of redlines and consequences could constitute a form of strategic ambiguity that gives the U.S. military operational maneuverability. Congress may wish to consider these concerns as new legislation regarding critical infrastructure protection is proposed.

Skilled cyber operators are in demand in the military, and the national supply of cyber professionals tends to reside in the private sector. Some of the services are looking at bolstering opportunities for officers who wish to pursue careers in cybersecurity by creating new occupational specialties and career tracks. Yet barriers to hiring skilled civilians for the DOD cyber mission may hinder the development of a robust workforce. Congress may choose to consider ways to incentivize and bolster recruitment of talent outside of the military, such as providing special hiring authorities for certain mission critical positions, streamlining or revising the clearance process for national security personnel, and compensation comparable to private sector equivalent jobs.

How Do DOD and Cyber Command Responsibilities for Cybersecurity Fit within the Interagency and Private Sector?

Reports have described the USCYBERCOM cyber force's "National Mission Teams" as protecting the networks that undergird critical infrastructure. Given that the majority of this critical infrastructure resides in the private sector, for which DHS has coordinating authority, how do USCYBERCOM teams protect these assets during peacetime without violating *Posse Comitatus*, the prohibition against using the military for domestic policing? How do these national teams interact and coordinate with DHS?

Should U.S. Cyber Command Be Its Own Unified Combatant Command?

The Unified Command Plan organizes combatant commands into geographic and functional areas. U.S. Cyber Command is currently organized under the functional Strategic Command, and co-directed and located with the National Security Agency (NSA). With the complicated lines of authority (Title 10 vs. Title 50) associated with this structure, some have suggested separating the two organizations and giving civilian control to the NSA while elevating Cyber Command to the level of a full unified combatant command. DOD has been tasked by Congress to study and report on the possible implications of this realignment. Specifically, The National Defense Authorization Act for Fiscal Year 2013 (P.L. 112-239) asks in Section 940 "how a single individual could serve as a commander of a combatant command that conducts overt, though clandestine, cyber operations under Title 10, United States Code, and serve as the head of an element of the intelligence community that conducts covert cyber operations under the National Security Act of 1947."

Is a Separate Cyber Force Necessary?

Given that the DOD views cyberspace as one of five global domains, some proponents in Congress contend that a separate cyber force, akin to the Army, Navy, Air Force, or Marine Corps, is necessary to properly address the military aspects of the domain. However, critics point to the multi-layered aspect of cyberspace in which all services have equities.

What Are the Authorizing and Oversight Committees and Jurisdictional Implications?

As previously discussed, blurred lines between operations undertaken under Title 10 and Title 50 authorities can complicate efforts to determine the chain of command and jurisdictional review process. What does this ambiguity mean for congressional oversight committees? Have some operations taken place without congressional notification? What has been the Department of Defense's role in responding to cyberattacks on private networks?

Current Legislation

The National Defense Authorization Act for Fiscal Year 2015 (P.L. 113-291) contains some provisions related to DOD cybersecurity and cyber operations. These provisions:

- require reporting on cyber incidents with respect to networks and information systems of operationally critical contractors and certain other contractors.
- require the Principal Cyber Advisor to identify improvements to ensure sufficient civilian workforce to support USCYBERCOM and components.
- direct a program of decryption to inspect content for threats and insider activity within DOD networks.
- state the Sense of Congress that as ICANN turns to global community for leadership, support should be given only if assurances are provided for current legacy IP numbers used by DOD and the U.S. government.
- direct that a new mission forces, training, manning and equipping plan and associated programmatic elements be submitted to Congress.
- state a Sense of Congress for consideration regarding role of reserve components in defense against cyberattacks given their unique experience in private and public sectors and existing relationships with local and civil authorities for emergency response.

APPENDIX. TIMELINE OF INTERNATIONAL ATTACKS[95]

February-June 1999: Kosovo was the arena for the first large-scale Internet war, involving pro-Serbian forces cyberattacking the North Atlantic Treaty Organization (NATO). As NATO planes bombed Serbia, pro-Serbian hacker groups, such as the "Black Hand," attacked NATO, U.S., and UK Internet infrastructure and computers via DoS attacks and virus-infected email. In the United States, the White House website was defaced. The UK admitted to losing database information. At NATO Headquarters in Belgium, a public affairs website for the war in Kosovo was "virtually inoperable for several days." Simultaneously, NATO's email server was flooded and choked with email.[96] During the Kosovo conflict, a NATO jet bombed the Chinese embassy in Belgrade in May 1999. The Chinese Red Hacker Alliance retaliated by launching thousands of cyberattacks against U.S. government websites. [97]

October 2000: Riots in the Palestinian territories sparked rounds of cyberattacks between Israelis and Palestinians. Pro-Israeli attacks targeted the official websites of the Palestinian Authority, Hamas, and the government of Iran. Pro-Palestinian hackers retaliated against Israeli political, military, telecommunications, media, the financial sector, commercial, and university websites. Since 2000, the Middle East cyberwar has kept pace with the ground conflict.[98]

April-May 2007: DDoS attacks shutdown websites of Estonia's parliament, banks, ministries, newspapers, and broadcasters. Estonian officials accused the Russian government of responding to their decision to move a Soviet-era war memorial with retaliatory cyberattacks.[99]

September 2007: Israel disrupted Syrian air defense networks during the bombing of an alleged nuclear facility in Syria.[100]

July 2008: Government and corporate websites in Lithuania were defaced. The Soviet-themed graffiti implicated Russian nationalist hackers.[101]

August 2008: Georgian government and commercial websites were shut down by DoS attacks at the same time that Russian ground troops invaded the country.[102]

January 2009: DoS attacks originating in Russia shut down Kyrgyzstan's two main Internet servers on the same day that the Russian government pressured Kyrgyzstan to bar U.S. access to a local airbase.[103]

July 2009: Servers in South Korea and the United States sustained a series of attacks, reportedly by North Korea.[104]

June 2010: "Stuxnet" worm damaged an Iranian nuclear facility. The United States and Israel were implicated in the attack.[105]

September 2011: "Keylogger" malware was found on ground control stations for U.S. Air Force unmanned aerial vehicles (UAVs) and reportedly infected both classified and unclassified networks at Creech Air Force Base in Nevada.

May 2012: An espionage worm called "Flame," allegedly 20 times more complex than Stuxnet, was discovered on computers in the Iranian Oil Ministry, as well as in Israel, Syria, and Sudan.

*August 2012***:** "Gauss" worm infected 2,500 systems worldwide. The malware appeared to have been aimed at Lebanese banks, and contained code whose encryption has not yet been broken.

August 2012: The "Cutting Sword of Justice," a group reportedly linked to the government of Iran, used the "Shamoon" virus to attack major oil companies including Aramco, a major Saudi oil supplier, and the Qatari company RasGas, a major liquefied natural gass (LNG) supplier. The attack on Aramco deleted data on 30,000 computers and infected (without causing damage) control systems.

September 2012-June 2013: The hacker group Izz ad-Din al-Qassam launched DoS attacks against major U.S. financial institutions in "Operation Ababil." Izz ad-Din al-Qassam is believed to have links to Iran and Hamas.

*January 2013***:** The *New York Times*, *Wall Street Journal*, *Washington Post*, and *Bloomberg News* revealed that they were targeted by persistent cyberattacks. China was the suspected source.

May 2013: Israeli officials reported a failed attempt by the Syrian Electronic Army to compromise water supply to the city of Haifa.

August 2013: Leaks revealed that the U.S. government purportedly conducted 231 cyber intrusions in 2011 against Russia, China, North Korea, and Iran. Most of the intrusions were related to nuclear proliferation.

April 2014: The disclosure of the Heartbleed bug revealed vulnerability in the OpenSSL protocol previously considered the standard for Internet security. Canada reported more than 900 compromised social security numbers.[106]

May 2014: The United States indicted five Chinese military officers on charges of computer hacking, economic espionage, and other offenses against six targets in the United States' nuclear power, metals, and solar power industries. China has denied the charges.[107] According to U.S. Attorney General Eric Holder, "This is a case alleging economic espionage by members of the Chinese military and represents the first ever charges against a state actor for this type of hacking."[108]

July 2014: The United States charged a Chinese entrepreneur with breaking into the computer systems of the U.S. defense giant Boeing and other firms to steal data on military programs concerning warplanes, including C-17 cargo aircraft, and the F-22 and F-35 fighter jets.[109] At the same time, the security firm Kapersky reported a massive cyber operation dubbed "Energetic Bear," which targeted more than 2,800 industrial firms around the globe. Although some reports identified a Russian hacker group as the source, Kapersky refrained from attributing the attack to any one country.[110]

December 2014: U.S. cybersecurity firm Cylance reported that an Iranian hacker group has breached airlines, energy and defense firms, and the U.S. Marine Corps intranet in an attack known as "Operation Cleaver."[111]

End Notes

[1] Information contained in this report is derived from unclassified open source material and discussions with senior government officials and industry technology and security experts.

[2] Crowd-sourcing refers to the use of online communities to obtain ideas, information, and services.

[3] Industrial espionage events are widely covered and notorious: attacks on Target, Home Depot, and Sony have caught national attention and have serious economic implications. Such events, however challenging, are not considered warfare for purposes of this report.

[4] Bruce Schneier, Schneier on Security (Indianapolis: Wiley, 2008); Michael Schmitt et al., Tallinn Manual on the Internationl Law Applicable to Cyber Warfare, prepared by the International Group of Experts at the invitation of the NATO Cooperative Cyber Defence Centre of Excellence, Cambridge: Cambridge University Press, 2013.

[5] Department of Defense Joint Publication 3-12, Cyberspace Operations, February 5, 2013.

[6] Ibid.

[7] Ibid.

[8] CRS Report R41524, The Stuxnet Computer Worm: Harbinger of an Emerging Warfare Capability, by Paul K. Kerr, John W. Rollins, and Catherine A. Theohary.

[9] Joshua Davis, "John McAfee Fled to Belize, But He Couldn't Escape Himself," Wired, December 24, 2012, http://www.wired.com/2012/12/ff-john-mcafees-last-stand/all.

[10] Chris Strohm, "Hedge-Fund Hack Part of Wall Street Siege Seen by Cyber-Experts," BloombergGovernment, June 23, 2014.

[11] Zheng Bu, Pedro Bueno, Rahul Kashyap, et al., The New Era of Botnets, McAfee: An Intel Company, white paper, Santa Clara, CA, 2010, pp. 3-4, http://www.mcafee.com/us/resources/white-papers/wp-new-era-of-botnets.pdf.

[12] John Markoff, "A Robot Network Seeks to Enlist Your Computer," New York Times, October 20, 2008.

[13] Richard A. Clark and Robert K. Knake, Cyber War: The Next Threat to National Security and What to Do about It (New York: HarperCollins, 2010), p. 13.

[14] Zheng Bu, Pedro Bueno, Rahul Kashyap, et al., The New Era of Botnets, McAfee: An Intel Company, White Paper, Santa Clara, CA, 2010, pp. 3-4, http://www.mcafee.com/us/resources/white-papers/wp-new-era-of-botnets.pdf.

[15] Ziv Gadot, Eyal Benishti, Lior Rozen, et al., Radware Global Application & Network Security Report 2012, Radware, White Paper, Mahwah, NJ, 2013, p. 1, file:///C:/Users/aharrington/Downloads/a7b991da-b96e-4cd7-bf8c236b1e7e4c67.pdf.

[16] Ziv Gadot, Eyal Benishti, Lior Rozen, et al., Radware Global Application & Network Security Report 2012, Radware, white paper, Mahwah, NJ, 2013, p. 18.

[17] http://www.root-servers.org/.

[18] 18 U.S.C. §1030.

[19] Ellen Nakashima, "Cyber-intruder sparks response, debate" Washington Post, December 8, 2011, http://www.washingtonpost.com/national/national-security/cyber-intruder-sparks-response-debate/2011/12/06/ gIQAxLuFgO_story.html.

[20] Critical Infrastructure is defined in 42 U.S.C. 5195c(e) as: "systems and assets, whether physical or virtual, so vital to the United States that the incapacity or destruction of such systems and assets would have a debilitating impact on security, national economic security, national public health or safety, or any combination of those matters."

[21] For additional information, see CRS Report RL31787, Information Operations, Cyberwarfare, and Cybersecurity: Capabilities and Related Policy Issues, by Catherine A. Theohary.

[22] For additional background information, see archived CRS Report RL33123, Terrorist Capabilities for Cyberattack: Overview and Policy Issues, by John W. Rollins and Clay Wilson.

[23] Accessed at http://intelreport.mandiant.com/Mandiant_APT1_Report.pdf.

[24] Peer-to-peer software refers to computer networks in which each computer can act as a server for the others, obviating the need for a central server for command and control.

[25] Joshua Davis, "Hackers Take Down the Most Wired Country in Europe," Wired, August 21, 2007, http://archive.wired.com/politics/security/magazine/15-09/ff_estonia?currentPage=all.

[26] Richard A. Clark and Robert Knake, Cyber War: The Next Threat to National Security and What to Do About It (New York: HarperCollins, 2010).

[27] Ibid.

[28] Peter Singer and Allan Friedman, Cybersecurity and Cyberwar: What Everyone Needs to Know (Oxford: Oxford University Press, 2013), pp. 110-111.

[29] Joshua Davis, "Hackers Take Down the Most Wired Country in Europe," Wired, August 21, 2007, http://archive.wired.com/politics/security/magazine/15-09/ff_estonia?currentPage=all.

[30] Ibid.

[31] Ibid.

[32] Martin C. Libicki, Conquest in Cyberspace: National Security and Information Warfare (Washington, DC: RAND, 2007).

[33] John Markoff, "Before the Gunfire, Cyberattacks," New York Times, August 12, 2008, http://www.nytimes.com/ 2008/08/13/technology/13cyber.html?_r=0.

[34] David Hollis, "Cyberwar Case Study: Georgia 2008," Small Wars Journal, January 6, 2011.

[35] For further discussion, see CRS Report RL34618, Russia-Georgia Conflict in August 2008: Context and Implications for U.S. Interests, by Jim Nichol

[36] Mikheil Saakashvili, "Let Georgia be a lesson for what will happen to Ukraine," The Guardian, March 14, 2014.

[37] Stephen W. Korns and Joshua E. Kastenberg, "Georgia's Cyber Left Hook," Parameters, Winter 2008, p. 65, http://strategicstudiesinstitute.army.mil/pubs/parameters/articles/08winter/korns.pdf.

[38] David Hollis, "Cyberwar Case Study: Georgia 2008 " Small Wars Journal, January 6, 2011, p.3

[39] Ibid.

[40] David Hollis, "Cyberwar Case Study: Georgia 2008," Small Wars Journal, January 6, 2011, p. 2.

[41] Stephen W. Korns and Joshua E. Kastenberg, "Georgia's Cyber Left Hook," Parameters, Winter 2008, p. 65, http://strategicstudiesinstitute.army.mil/pubs/parameters/articles/08winter/korns.pdf.

[42] David Hollis, "Cyberwar Case Study: Georgia 2008," Small Wars Journal, January 6, 2011, p. 4.

[43] P. Mittal, "How Digital Detectives Deciphered Stuxnet, the Most Menacing Malware in History," Wired, July 11, 2011, http://www.wired.com/2011/07/how-digital-detectives-deciphered-stuxnet/all/.

[44] In his memoir, Thomas Reed, a former U.S. Air Force secretary who served in the National Security Council during President Reagan's tenure, describes a successful CIA plot to sabotage the Soviet Union's Siberian pipeline in 1982 by tricking Moscow into stealing booby-trapped software. The faulty ICS software overpressurized the system causing "the most monumental non-nuclear explosion and fire ever seen from space." Alec Russell, "CIA plot led to huge blast in Siberian gas pipeline" The Telegraph, February 28, 2004, http://www.telegraph.co.uk/news/worldnews/northamerica/usa/1455559/CIA-plot-led-to-huge-blast-in-Siberian-gas-pipeline.html; Michael Joseph Gross, "A Declaration of Cyber-War," Wired, April 2011, http://www.vanityfair.com/culture/features/2011/04/stuxnet-201104.

[45] Eventually, specialists identified over 100, 000 corrupted devices. For more see P. Mittal, "How Digital Detectives Deciphered Stuxnet, the Most Menacing Malware in History," Wired, July 11, 2011, http://www.wired.com/2011/07/ how-digital-detectives-deciphered-stuxnet/all/; Ralph Langer, "To Kill a Centrifuge: A Technical Analysis of What Stuxnet's Creators Tried to Achieve," November, 2013, http://www.langner.com/en/wp-content/uploads/2013/11/Tokill-a-centrifuge.pdf; William J. Broad, John Markoff, and David Sanger, "Israeli Test on Worm Called Crucial in Iran Nuclear Delay," New York Times, January 15, 2011, http://www.nytimes.com/2011/01/16/world/middleeast/16stuxnet.html?pagewanted=all&_r=0; Paul Kerr, John Rollins and Catherine Theohary, "The Stuxnet Computer Worm: Harbinger of an Emerging Warfare Capability," Congressional Research Service Report, December 9, 2010.

[46] P. Mittal, "How Digital Detectives Deciphered Stuxnet, the Most Menacing Malware in History," Wired, July 11, 2011, http://www.wired.com/2011/07/how-digital-detectives-deciphered-stuxnet/all/.

[47] Anne Harrington and Matthias Englert, "How Much is Enough? The Politics of Technology and Weaponless Nuclear Deterrence" in International Relations and the Global Politics of Science and Technology, eds. Mariana Carpes and Maximilian Mayer, Berlin: Springer, 2014.

[48] The cybersecurity company Symantec has since established that there were multiple variants of Stuxnet. The earlier variant closed valves, causing a build-up of pressure that will make the centrifuge wobble and damage the rotors, rather than directly affecting the rate at which the centrifuge spins. For more, see Institute for Science and International Security, Basic Attack

Strategy of Stuxnet 0.5 rev. 1, Institute for Science and International Security, Washington, DC, February 28, 2013, http://isis-online.org/isis-reports/detail/basic-attack-strategy-of-stuxnet-0.5/.

[49] Dr. Fereydoun Abassi, Vice President of the Islamic Republic of Iran and Head of Atomic Energy Organization of Iran, "Statement at the IAEA 56th General Conference," September 17, 2012; P. Mittal, "How Digital Detectives Deciphered Stuxnet, the Most Menacing Malware in History," Wired, July 11, 2011, pp. http://www.wired.com/2011/ 07/how-digital-detectives-deciphered-stuxnet/all/.

[50] David Albright and Christina Walrond, Performance of the IR-1 Centrifuge at Natanz, Institute for Science and International Security, Washington, DC, October 18, 2011, http://isis-online.org/isis-reports/detail/test1/8.

[51] William J. Broad, John Markoff, and David Sanger, "Israeli Test on Worm Called Crucial in Iran Nuclear Delay," New York Times, January 15, 2011, http://www.nytimes.com/2011/01/16/world/middleeast/16stuxnet.html? pagewanted=all&_r=0.

[52] Source: Internal Department of Defense budget documents.

[53] Advanced Questions for Vice Admiral Michael S. Rogers, Nominee for Commander, United States Cyber Command, Senate Armed Services Hearing of March 11, 2014, http://www.armed-services.senate.gov/imo/media/doc/ Rogers_03-11-14.pdf.

[54] From http://www.washingtonpost.com/world/national-security/pentagon-to-boost-cyber security-force/2013/01/27/ d87d9dc2-5fec-11e2-b05a-605528f6b712_story.html.

[55] http://www.defensenews.com/article/20141103/TRAINING/311030018/As-cyber-force-grow s-manpower-detailsemerge.

[56] Wyatt Olson, "Cyber Command trying to get running start, add staff," Stars and Stripes, December 11, 2014.

[57] DOD Dictionary of Military and Associated Terms, JP1-02.

[58] U.S. Military Given Secret "Execute Order" on Cyber Operations Military Doctrine, Secrecy http://blogs.fas.org/secrecy/2014/03/execute-order/.

[59] The previous version would have given the Secretary of Defense the authority to conduct clandestine cyberspace activities in support of military operations pursuant specifically to the Authorization for the Use of Military Force (P.L. 107-40; 50 U.S.C. 1541 note) outside of the United States or to defend against a cyberattack on an asset of the Department of Defense.

[60] Department of Defense Dictionary of Military and Associated Terms, Joint Publication1-02, as amended through August 15, 2014. [reconcile with similar footnote above]

[61] "Report: White House should oversee cybersecurity," CNN, December 8, 2008, http://www.cnn.com/2008/TECH/12/ 08/cyber.security/.

[62] The White House, "President Obama Directs the National Security and Homeland Security Advisors to Conduct Immediate Cyber Security Review," press release, February 9, 2009, http://www.whitehouse.gov/the-press-office/ president-obama-directs-national-security-and-homeland-security-advisors-conduct-im.

[63] The White House, Cyberspace Policy Review, May 29, 2009, http://www.whitehouse.gov/assets/documents/ Cyberspace_Policy_Review_final.pdf; the White House, "Cyberspace Policy Review [Supporting Documents]," May 2009, http://www. whitehouse.gov/cyberreview/documents/.

[64] The White House, "Remarks by the President on Securing Our Nation's Cyber Infrastructure," press release, May 29, 2009, http://www.whitehouse.gov/the_press_office/Remarks-by-the-President-on-Securing-Our-Nations-CyberInfrastructure/.

[65] CRS Report R41674, Terrorist Use of the Internet: Information Operations in Cyberspace, by Catherine A. Theohary and John W. Rollins; CRS Report R42507, Cybersecurity: Authoritative Reports and Resources, by Topic, by Rita Tehan.

[66] "The Comprehensive National Cybersecurity Initiative," http://www.whitehouse.gov/ issues/foreign-policy/ cybersecurity/national-initiative; National Security Presidential Directive 54 / Homeland Security Presidential Directive 23 (NSPD-54/HSPD-23).

[67] CRS Report R40427, Comprehensive National Cybersecurity Initiative: Legal Authorities and Policy Considerations, by John W. Rollins and Anna C. Henning.

[68] Joshua Eaton, "American cyber-attack list uncovered," Al Jazeera, http://america.aljazeera. com/articles/multimedia/ timeline-edward-snowden-revelations.html, accessed August 12, 2014.

[69] Ellen Nakashima, "Obama Signs Secret Directive to Help Thwart Cyberattacks" Washington Post, November 14, 2012.

[70] Cheryl Pellerin, "DOD Readiness Elements Crucial to Cyber Operations" U.S. Department of Defense, American Forces Press Service, http://www.defense.gov/ news/newsarticle. aspx?id=120381.

[71] The White House, "Critical Infrastructure Security and Resilience," Presidential Policy Directive 21, February 12, 2013, http://www.whitehouse.gov/the-press-office/2013/02/ 12/presidential-policy-directive-critical-infrastructuresecurity-and-resil.

[72] Department of Homeland Security, National Cyber Incident Response Plan, Interim Version, September 2010.

[73] Accessed at https://www.dhs.gov/xlibrary/assets/20101013-dod-dhs-cyber-moa.pdf.

[74] The White House, International Strategy for Cyberspace, May 2011, http://www.whitehouse. gov/sites/default/files/ rss_viewer/international_strategy_for_cyberspace.pdf.

[75] Remarks of Harold Hongju Koh, Legal Advisor U.S. Department of State, at a USCYBERCOM Inter-Agency Legal Conference, Ft. Meade, MD, September 18, 2012.

[76] Jack Goldsmith, "Cybersecurity Treaties: A Skeptical View" Future Challenges Essay, June 2, 2011, http://media.hoover.org/sites/default/files/documents/FutureChallenges_ Goldsmith. pdf. He cites "vague definitions," reservations by signatories, and loopholes as reasons for its lack of success.

[77] Council of Europe, "Convention on Cybercrime, CETS No. 185," accessed February 18, 2013, http://conventions.coe.int/Treaty/Commun/ChercheSig.asp?NT=185&CM=8& DF= &CL=ENG. See also Michael Vatis, "The Council of Europe Convention on Cybercrime," in Proceedings of a Workshop on Deterring CyberAttacks: Informing Strategies and Developing Options for U.S. Policy (Washington, DC: National Academies Press, 2010), pp. 207–223.

[78] The abbreviation ICT, which stands for information and communications technologies, is increasingly used instead of IT, (information technologies) because of the convergence of telecommunications and computer technology.

[79] United Nations General Assembly, Report of the Group of Governmental Experts on Developments in the Field of Information and Telecommunications in the Context of International Security, July 30, 2010, http://www.un.org/ga/ search/view_ doc.asp?symbol =A/65/201.

[80] Oona Hathaway et al., "The Law of Cyber-Attack," California Law Review 100, no. 4 (2012), http://papers.ssrn.com/ sol3/papers.cfm?abstract_id=2134932.

[81] For a detailed discussion, see Hathaway et al., "The Law of Cyber-Attack." See also CRS Report RL31787, Information Operations, Cyberwarfare, and Cybersecurity: Capabilities and Related Policy Issues, by Catherine A. Theohary; James A. Lewis, Conflict and

Negotiation in Cyberspace (Center for Strategic and International Studies, February 2013), https://csis.org/files/publication/130208_Lewis_ConflictCyberspace_Web.pdf; Mary Ellen O'Connell and Louise Arimatsu, Cyber Security and International Law (London, UK: Chatham House, May 29, 2012), http://www.tsa.gov/sites/default/files/assets/pdf/Intermodal/pipeline_sec_incident_recvr_protocol_plan.pdf.

[82] Hathaway et al., "The Law of Cyber-Attack," p. 857.

[83] See CRS Report RL31787, Information Operations, Cyberwarfare, and Cybersecurity: Capabilities and Related Policy Issues, by Catherine A. Theohary.

[84] The concept document (available at http://www.nato.int/cps/en/natolive/ official _texts_ 68580.htm) states that NATO will "develop further our ability to prevent, detect, defend against and recover from cyber-attacks, including by using the NATO planning process to enhance and coordinate national cyberdefence capabilities, bringing all NATO bodies under centralized cyber protection, and better integrating NATO cyber awareness, warning and response with member nations."

[85] North Atlantic Treaty Organization, "NATO and Cyber Defence," February 19, 2013, http://www.nato.int/cps/en/ SID-537741AA-89F4BEF4/natolive/topics_78170.htm?.

[86] Hathaway et al., "The Law of Cyber-Attack." See also Anthony Rutkowski, "Public International Law of the International Telecommunication Instruments: Cyber Security Treaty Provisions Since 1850," Info 13, no. 1 (2011): 13–31, http://www. emeraldinsight. com/journals.htm?issn=1463-6697&volume=13&issue=1&articleid=1893240&show= pdf&PHPSESSID=9r0c5maa4spkkd9li78ugbjee3.

[87] Hathaway et al., "The Law of Cyber-Attack."

[88] See, for example, Lolita Baldor, "Cyber Security Added to US-Australia Treaty," Security on NBCNews.com, 2011, http://www.msnbc.msn.com/id/44527648/ns/ technology_and_ science-security/t/cyber-security-added-us-australiatreaty/.

[89] For summaries, see International Telecommunication Union, Global Cybersecurity Agenda (GCA): Global Strategic Report, 2008, http://www.itu.int/osg/csd/cybersecurity/gca/ global_strategic_report/global_strategic_report.pdf.

[90] Ministry of Foreign Affairs of the People's Republic of China, "China, Russia and Other Countries Submit the Document of International Code of Conduct for Information Security to the United Nations," September 13, 2011, http://www.fmprc.gov.cn/ eng/zxxx/t858978. htm.

[91] Among the concerns cited were the absence of provisions on international law enforcement and combating cyberespionage; its call for international cooperation relating to "curbing dissemination of information" relating to "political, economic, and social stability" and "spiritual and cultural environment"; and ambiguity with respect to censorship policy (Jeffrey Carr, "4 Problems with China and Russia's International Code of Conduct for Information Security," Digital Dao, September 22, 2011, http://jeffreycarr.blogspot.com/ 2011/09/4-problems-with-china-andrussias.html).

[92] Aliya Sternstein, "U.S., Russia, Other Nations Near Agreement on Cyber Early-Warning Pact," Nextgov: Cybersecurity, December 5, 2012, http://www.nextgov.com/cybersecurity/ 2012/12/us-russia-other-nations-nearagreement-cyber-early-warning-pact/59977/; Aliya Sternstein, "Cyber Early Warning Deal Collapses After Russia Balks," Nextgov: Cybersecurity, December 7, 2012, http://www.nextgov.com/cybersecurity/2012/12/cyber-earlywarning-deal-collapses-after-russia-balks/60035/.

[93] Goldsmith, "Cybersecurity Treaties: A Skeptical View."

[94] Deep packet inspection allows the content of a unit of data to be examined as it travels through an inspection point, a process which enables data mining and eavesdropping programs.

[95] Unless otherwise noted, these events are cited in "Significant Cyber Events" Washington, DC: Center for Strategic and International Studies, http://csis.org/program/significant-cyber-events; accessed August 7, 2014.

[96] Kenneth Geers, "Cyberspace and the Changing Nature of Warfare," keynote speech, Japan, 2008, http://www.blackhat.com/presentations/bh-jp-08/bh-jp-08-Geers/BlackHat-Japan-08-Geers-Cyber-WarfareWhitepaper.pdf.

[97] Jeffrey Carr, "Real Cyber Warfare: Carr's Top Five Picks," Forbes, February 4, 2011, http://www.forbes.com/sites/jeffreycarr/2011/02/04/real-cyber-warfare-carrs-top-five-picks/; Kenneth Geers, "Cyberspace and the Changing Nature of Warfare," keynote speech, Japan, 2008, http://www.blackhat.com/presentations/bh-jp-08/bh-jp-08-Geers/BlackHat-Japan-08-Geers-Cyber-Warfare-Whitepaper.pdf.

[98] Kenneth Geers, "Cyberspace and the Changing Nature of Warfare," keynote speech, Japan, 2008, http://www.blackhat.com/presentations/bh-jp-08/bh-jp-08-Geers/BlackHat-Japan-08-Geers-Cyber-WarfareWhitepaper.pdf.

[99] Joshua Davis, "Hackers Take Down the Most Wired Country in Europe," Wired, August 21, 2007, http://archive.wired.com/politics/security/magazine/15-09/ff_estonia?currentPage =all.

[100] "Significant Cyber Events" Washington, DC: Center for Strategic and International Studies, http://csis.org/program/ significant-cyber-events; accessed August 7, 2014.

[101] Brian Krebs, "Lithuania Weathers Cyberattack, Braces for Round 2," The Washington Post, July 3, 2008, http://voices.washingtonpost.com/securityfix/2008/07/lithuania_ weathers_ cyber_attac_1.html.

[102] John Markoff, "Before the Gunfire, Cyberattacks," New York Times, August 12, 2008, http://www.nytimes.com/ 2008/08/13/technology/13cyber.html?_r=0.

[103] Daniel McLaughlin, "Lithuania accuses Russian hackers of cyber assault after collapse of over 300 websites" (Irish Times, July 2, 2008) p. 10, http://lumen.cgsccarl.com/login?url= http://proquest.umi.com/pqdweb? did=1503762091&sid=2&Fmt=3&cl ientld=5094 &RQT=309&VName=PQD.

[104] "Significant Cyber Events" Washington, DC: Center for Strategic and International Studies, http://csis.org/program/ significant-cyber-events; accessed August 7, 2014.

[105] Ralph Langer, "To Kill a Centrifuge: A Technical Analysis of What Stuxnet's Creators Tried to Achieve," November, 2013, http://www.langner.com/en/wp-content/uploads/2013/11/To-kill-a-centrifuge.pdf.

[106] http://heartbleed.com/; "OpenSSL Heartbleed Vulnerability" Cyber Security Bulletins. Public Safety Canada. April 11, 2014, retrieved April 14, 2014. SSL (Secure Sockets Layer) is the standard security technology for establishing an encrypted link between a web server and a browser.

[107] Song Sang-ho, "Concerns rise over militarization of cyberspace," The Korean Herald, July 13, 2014, http://www.koreaherald.com/view.php?ud=20140713000188.

[108] Office of Public Affairs, U.S. Charges Five Chinese Military Hackers for Cyber Espionage Against U.S. Corporations and a Labor Organization for Commercial Advantage, Department of Justice, May 19, 2014, http://www.justice.gov/opa/pr/2014/May/14-ag-528.html.

[109] Dan Levine, "US Charges Chinese Man with Hacking into Boeing," Reuters, July 11, 2014, http://www.reuters.com/article/2014/07/11/boeing-china-cybercrime-idUSL2N0PM2FV20140711.; Song Sang-ho, "Concerns rise over militarization of cyberspace," The Korean Herald, July 13, 2014, http://www.koreaherald.com/ view.php?ud=20140713000188.

[110] See http://www.darkreading.com/attacks-breaches/energetic-bear-under-the-microscope/d/d-id/1297712.

[111] See http://www.defensenews.com/article/20141202/DEFREG04/312020030/Report-Iran-Hackers-InfiltratedAirlines-Energy-Defense-Firms.

In: Cyberspace Threat Landscape
Editor: Cody L. Barker
ISBN: 978-1-63482-338-8

Chapter 2

CYBERSECURITY ISSUES AND CHALLENGES: IN BRIEF*

Eric A. Fischer

SUMMARY

The information and communications technology (ICT) industry has evolved greatly over the last half century. The technology is ubiquitous and increasingly integral to almost every facet of modern society. ICT devices and components are generally interdependent, and disruption of one may affect many others. Over the past several years, experts and policy makers have expressed increasing concerns about protecting ICT systems from cyberattacks, which many experts expect to increase in frequency and severity over the next several years.

The act of protecting ICT systems and their contents has come to be known as cybersecurity. A broad and arguably somewhat fuzzy concept, cybersecurity can be a useful term but tends to defy precise definition. It is also sometimes inappropriately conflated with other concepts such as privacy, information sharing, intelligence gathering, and surveillance. However, cybersecurity can be an important tool in protecting privacy and preventing unauthorized surveillance, and information sharing and intelligence gathering can be useful tools for effecting cybersecurity.

* This is an edited, reformatted and augmented version of a Congressional Research Service publication R43831, prepared for Members and Committees of Congress, dated December 16, 2014.

The management of risk to information systems is considered fundamental to effective cybersecurity. The risks associated with any attack depend on three factors: threats (who is attacking), vulnerabilities (how they are attacking), and impacts (what the attack does). Most cyberattacks have limited impacts, but a successful attack on some components of critical infrastructure (CI)—most of which is held by the private sector—could have significant effects on national security, the economy, and the livelihood and safety of individual citizens. Reducing such risks usually involves removing threat sources, addressing vulnerabilities, and lessening impacts.

The federal role in cybersecurity involves both securing federal systems and assisting in protecting nonfederal systems. Under current law, all federal agencies have cybersecurity responsibilities relating to their own systems, and many have sector-specific responsibilities for CI. On average, federal agencies spend more than 10% of their annual ICT budgets on cybersecurity.

More than 50 statutes address various aspects of cybersecurity, and new legislation has been debated since at least the 111th Congress. Executive Order 13636 and Presidential Policy Directive 21, released in February 2013, address the cybersecurity of CI through voluntary public/private sector collaboration and use of existing regulatory authorities. Four bills enacted in December 2014 address the security of federal ICT, the cybersecurity workforce at the Department of Homeland Security (DHS), and DHS information-sharing activities. Other bills would address information sharing more broadly, research and development, protection of CI, notification of victims of data breaches, and cybercrime laws, among other issues.

The executive-branch actions and proposed legislation are largely designed to address several well-established near-term needs in cybersecurity. However, those needs exist in the context of more difficult long-term challenges relating to design, incentives, consensus, and environment. Legislation and executive actions in the 114th Congress could have significant impacts on those challenges.

The information technology (IT) industry has evolved greatly over the last half century. Continued, exponential progress in processing power and memory capacity has made IT hardware not only faster, but also smaller, light, cheaper, and easier to use.

The original IT industry has also increasingly converged with the communications industry into a combined sector commonly called information and communications technology (ICT). This technology is ubiquitous and increasingly integral to almost every facet of modern society. ICT devices and components are generally interdependent, and disruption of one may affect many others.

THE CONCEPT OF CYBERSECURITY

Over the past several years, experts and policy makers have expressed increasing concerns about protecting ICT systems from *cyberattacks*—deliberate attempts by unauthorized persons to access ICT systems, usually with the goal of theft, disruption, damage, or other unlawful actions. Many experts expect the number and severity of cyberattacks to increase over the next several years.[1]

The act of protecting ICT systems and their contents has come to be known as *cybersecurity*. A broad and arguably somewhat fuzzy concept, cybersecurity can be a useful term but tends to defy precise definition. It usually refers to one or more of three things:

- A set of activities and other measures intended to protect—from attack, disruption, or other threats—computers, computer networks, related hardware and devices software, and the information they contain and communicate, including software and data, as well as other elements of cyberspace.[2]
- The state or quality of being protected from such threats.
- The broad field of endeavor aimed at implementing and improving those activities and quality.[3]

It is related to but not generally regarded as identical to the concept of information security, which is defined in federal law (44 U.S.C. §3542(b)(1)) as

> protecting information and information systems from unauthorized access, use, disclosure, disruption, modification, or destruction in order to provide-
>
> (A) integrity, which means guarding against improper information modification or destruction, and includes ensuring information nonrepudiation and authenticity;
>
> (B) confidentiality, which means preserving authorized restrictions on access and disclosure, including means for protecting personal privacy and proprietary information; and

(C) availability, which means ensuring timely and reliable access to and use of information.

Cybersecurity is also sometimes conflated inappropriately in public discussion with other concepts such as privacy, information sharing, intelligence gathering, and surveillance. Privacy is associated with the ability of an individual person to control access by others to information about that person. Thus, good cybersecurity can help protect privacy in an electronic environment, but information that is shared to assist in cybersecurity efforts might sometimes contain personal information that at least some observers would regard as private. Cybersecurity can be a means of protecting against undesired surveillance of and gathering of intelligence from an information system. However, when aimed at potential sources of cyberattacks, such activities can also be useful to help effect cybersecurity. In addition, surveillance in the form of monitoring of information flow within a system can be an important component of cybersecurity.[4]

Management of Cybersecurity Risks

The risks associated with any attack depend on three factors: *threats* (who is attacking), *vulnerabilities* (how they are attacking), and *impacts* (what the attack does). The management of risk to information systems is considered fundamental to effective cybersecurity.[5]

What Are the Threats?

People who perform cyberattacks generally fall into one or more of five categories: *criminals* intent on monetary gain from crimes such as theft or extortion; *spies* intent on stealing classified or proprietary information used by government or private entities; *nation-state warriors* who develop capabilities and undertake cyberattacks in support of a country's strategic objectives; "*hacktivists*" who perform cyberattacks for nonmonetary reasons; and *terrorists* who engage in cyberattacks as a form of non-state or state-sponsored warfare.

What Are the Vulnerabilities?

Cybersecurity is in many ways an arms race between attackers and defenders. ICT systems are very complex, and attackers are constantly probing for weaknesses, which can occur at many points. Defenders can often protect against weaknesses, but three are particularly challenging: inadvertent or intentional acts by *insiders* with access to a system; *supply chain* vulnerabilities, which can permit the insertion of malicious software or hardware during the acquisition process; and previously unknown, or *zero-day*, vulnerabilities with no established fix.

What Are the Impacts?

A successful attack can compromise the confidentiality, integrity, and availability of an ICT system and the information it handles. *Cybertheft* or *cyberespionage* can result in exfiltration of financial, proprietary, or personal information from which the attacker can benefit, often without the knowledge of the victim. *Denial-of-service* attacks can slow or prevent legitimate users from accessing a system. *Botnet* malware can give an attacker command of a system for use in cyberattacks on other systems. Attacks on *industrial control systems* can result in the destruction of the equipment they control, such as generators, pumps, and centrifuges.

Most cyberattacks have limited impacts, but a successful attack on some components of critical infrastructure (CI)—most of which is held by the private sector—could have significant effects on national security, the economy, and the livelihood and safety of individual citizens. Thus, a rare successful attack with high impact can pose a larger risk than a common successful attack with low impact.

Reducing the risks from cyberattacks usually involves (1) removing the threat source (e.g., by closing down botnets or reducing incentives for cybercriminals); (2) addressing vulnerabilities by hardening ICT assets (e.g., by patching software and training employees); and (3) lessening impacts by mitigating damage and restoring functions (e.g., by having back-up resources available for continuity of operations in response to an attack).

FEDERAL ROLE

The federal role in cybersecurity involves both securing federal systems and assisting in protecting nonfederal systems. Under current law, all federal agencies have cybersecurity responsibilities relating to their own systems, and many have sector-specific responsibilities for CI. More than 50 statutes address various aspects of cybersecurity, and new legislation has been debated since at least the 111th Congress. However, until the end of the 113th Congress, no bills on cybersecurity had been enacted since the Federal Information Security Management Act (FISMA) in 2002.

Figure 1 is a simplified schematic diagram of major agency responsibilities in cybersecurity. In general, the National Institute of Standards and Technology (NIST) develops FISMA standards that apply to federal civilian ICT, and the Office of Management and Budget (OMB) is responsible for overseeing their implementation. The Department of Defense (DOD) is responsible for military cyberdefense and, through the National Security Agency (NSA), security of national security systems (NSS), which handle classified information. NSA is also part of the Intelligence Community (IC). The Department of Homeland Security (DHS) has operational responsibility for protection of federal civilian systems and is the lead agency coordinating federal efforts assisting the private sector in protecting CI assets under their control. The Department of Justice (DOJ) is the lead agency for enforcement of relevant laws.

Executive Order 13636

In February 2013, the White House issued Executive Order 13636 and Presidential Policy Directive 21 to address CI cybersecurity through voluntary public/private sector collaboration and use of existing regulatory authorities. Among other things, the documents expanded an existing DHS information-sharing program and required NIST to lead public/private development of a Cybersecurity Framework of standards and best practices for protecting CI. Released in February 2014, the Framework received positive reviews, but it appears too early to determine the extent to which it will improve CI cybersecurity.

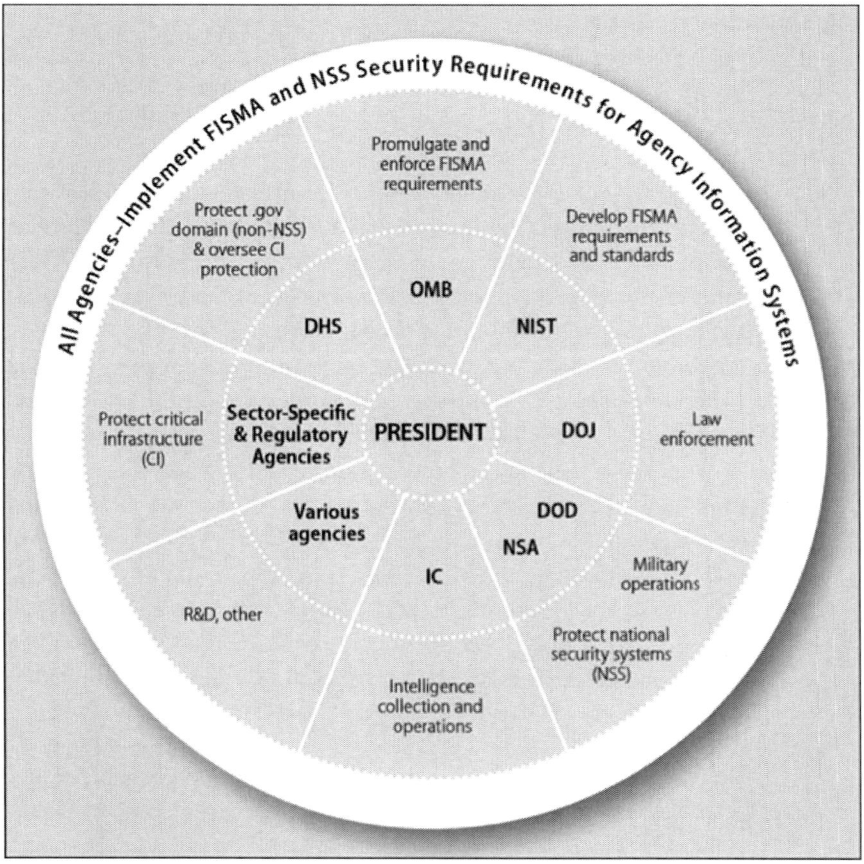

Source: CRS

Notes: DHS: Department of Homeland Security; DOD: Department of Defense; DOJ: Department of Justice; FISMA: Federal Information Security Management Act; IC: Intelligence Community; NIST: National Institute of Standards and Technology; NSA: National Security Agency; OMB: Office of Management and Budget; R&D: Research and development.

Figure 1. Simplified Schematic Diagram of Federal Agency Cybersecurity Roles.

Federal agencies spend a significant part of their annual IT funding on cybersecurity, which currently constitutes more than one in every eight dollars of agency IT budgets (*Table 1*).

Legislative Proposals

Since the 111th Congress, many bills have been introduced that would address cybersecurity issues. The main issues addressed by the bills are

- *Information Sharing*—easing access of the private sector to classified threat information and removing barriers to sharing within the private sector and with the federal government. *Controversies:* Roles of DHS and the IC, impacts on privacy and civil liberties, and risks of misuse by the federal government or the private sector.
- *FISMA Reform*—updating the 2002 law to reflect changes in ICT and the threat landscape. *Controversies:* Role of DHS, OMB, and Commerce, and flexibility of requirements.
- *R&D*—updating agency authorizations and strategic planning requirements. *Controversies:* Agency roles, topics for R&D, and levels of funding.
- *Workforce*—improving the size, skills, and preparation of the federal and private-sector cybersecurity workforce. *Controversies:* Hiring and retention authorities, occupational classification, recruitment priorities, and roles of DHS, NSA, the National Science Foundation (NSF), and NIST.
- *Privately Held CI*—improving protection of private-sector CI from attacks with major impacts. *Controversies:* Roles of DHS and other federal agencies, and regulatory vs. voluntary approach.
- *Data-Breach Notification*—requiring notification to victims and other responses after data breaches involving personal or financial information of individuals. *Controversies:* Federal vs. state roles and what responses should be required.
- *Cybercrime Laws*—updating criminal statutes and law-enforcement authorities relating to cybersecurity. *Controversies:* Adequacy of current penalties and authorities, impacts on privacy and civil liberties.

Four bills—on FISMA reform (S. 2521), the DHS cybersecurity workforce (H.R. 2952 and S. 1691), and a DHS information sharing center (S. 2519)—were enacted in December 2014.

Table 1. Federal FISMA and IT Spending Billions of Dollars, FY2006 to FY2013

Fiscal Year	2006	2007	2008	2009	2010	2011	2012	2013
FISMA Spending	5.5	5.9	6.2	6.8	12.0	13.3	14.6	10.3
Total IT Spending	66.2	68.2	72.8	76.1	80.7	76.0	75.0	73.2
FISMA Proportion of Total IT	8.3	8.7	8.5	8.9	14.9	17.5	19.5	13.8
Spending (%)								

Source: Data on FISMA spending are from annual reports on implementation of FISMA from the Office of Management and Budget (OMB), many of which are available at http://www.whitehouse.gov/omb/e-gov/docs. Data on total IT spending are from OMB Exhibit 53 spreadsheets (see Office of Management and Budget, "Exhibit 53 Archive," Federal IT Dashboard, August 31, 2014, https://itdashboard.gov/exhibit53report for recent documents).

Notes: FISMA data for FY2006-FY2009 are not comparable to later data, and data from 2013 are not comparable to earlier data, because of changes in how OMB collected the information. Amounts for both FISMA and IT spending are reported in the documents as "actual" expenditures and therefore probably consist mostly of obligated funds. Federal documents provide data as IT, not ICT, spending, but include investments in activities such as telecommunications (Office of Management and Budget, "Guidance on Exhibit 53—Information Technology and E-Government," August 5, 2011, http://www.whitehouse.gov/sites/default/files/omb/assets/ egov_docs/fy13_guidance_for_exhibit_53-a-b_20110805.pdf).

LONG-TERM CHALLENGES

The executive-branch actions and proposed legislation are largely designed to address several well-established near-term needs in cybersecurity: preventing cyber-based disasters and espionage, reducing impacts of successful attacks, improving inter- and intrasector collaboration, clarifying federal agency roles and responsibilities, and fighting cybercrime. However, those needs exist in the context of more difficult long-term challenges relating to design, incentives, consensus, and environment (DICE):

Design: Experts often say that effective security needs to be an integral part of ICT design. Yet, developers have traditionally focused more on features than security, for economic reasons. Also, many future security needs cannot be predicted, posing a difficult challenge for designers.

Incentives: The structure of economic incentives for cybersecurity has been called distorted or even perverse. Cybercrime is regarded as cheap, profitable, and comparatively safe for the criminals. In contrast, cybersecurity can be expensive, is by its nature imperfect, and the economic returns on investments are often unsure.

Consensus: Cybersecurity means different things to different stakeholders, with little common agreement on meaning, implementation, and risks. Substantial cultural impediments to consensus also exist, not only between sectors but within sectors and even within organizations.

Environment: Cyberspace has been called the fastest evolving technology space in human history, both in scale and properties. New and emerging properties and applications—especially social media, mobile computing, big data, cloud computing, and the Internet of things—further complicate the evolving threat environment, but they can also pose potential opportunities for improving cybersecurity, for example through the economies of scale provided by cloud computing and big data analytics.

Legislation and executive actions in the 114th Congress could have significant impacts on those challenges. For example, cybersecurity R&D may affect the design of ICT, cybercrime penalties may influence the structure of incentives, the Framework may improve consensus about cybersecurity, and federal initiatives in cloud computing and other new components of cyberspace may help shape the evolution of cybersecurity.

End Notes

[1] See, for example, Lee Rainie, Janna Anderson, and Jennifer Connolly, Cyber Attacks Likely to Increase (Pew Research Internet Project, October 2014), http://www.pewInternet.org/2014/10/29/cyber-attacks-likely-to-increase/.

[2] The term cyberspace usually refers to the worldwide collection of connected ICT components, the information that is stored in and flows through those components, and the ways that information is structured and processed.

[3] For a more in-depth discussion of this concept, see CRS Report RL32777, Creating a National Framework for Cybersecurity: An Analysis of Issues and Options, by Eric A. Fischer.

[4] See, for example, Department of Homeland Security, "Continuous Diagnostics and Mitigation (CDM)," June 24, 2014, http://www.dhs.gov/cdm.

[5] See, for example, National Institute of Standards and Technology, Managing Information Security Risk: Organization, Mission, and Information System View, March 2011, http://csrc.nist.gov/publications/nistpubs/800-39/ SP800-39-final.pdf.

In: Cyberspace Threat Landscape
Editor: Cody L. Barker

ISBN: 978-1-63482-338-8

Chapter 3

THE 2013 CYBERSECURITY EXECUTIVE ORDER: OVERVIEW AND CONSIDERATIONS FOR CONGRESS*

Eric A. Fischer, Edward C. Liu,
John W. Rollins and Catherine A. Theohary

SUMMARY

The federal role in cybersecurity has been a topic of discussion and debate for over a decade. Despite significant legislative efforts in the 112th Congress on bills designed to improve the cybersecurity of U.S. critical infrastructure (CI), no legislation on that issue was enacted in that Congress. In an effort to address the issue in the absence of enacted legislation, the White House issued an executive order in February 2013. Citing repeated cyber-intrusions into critical infrastructure and growing cyberthreats, Executive Order 13636, *Improving Critical Infrastructure Cybersecurity,* was an attempt to enhance security and resiliency of CI through voluntary, collaborative efforts involving federal agencies and owners and operators of privately owned CI, as well as use of existing federal regulatory authorities.

Entities posing a significant threat to the cybersecurity of CI assets include cyberterrorists, cyberspies, cyberthieves, cyberwarriors, and

* This is an edited, reformatted and augmented version of a Congressional Research Service publication R42984, prepared for Members and Committees of Congress, dated December 15, 2014.

cyberhacktivists. E.O. 13636 has attempted to address such threats by, among other things,

- expanding to other CI sectors an existing Department of Homeland Security (DHS) program for information sharing and collaboration between the government and the private sector;
- establishing a broadly consultative process for identifying CI with especially high priority for protection;
- requiring the National Institute of Standards and Technology (NIST) to lead in developing a cybersecurity framework of standards and best practices for protecting CI; and
- directing regulatory agencies to determine the adequacy of existing requirements and their authority to establish additional ones to address the risks.

Among the major issues covered by the unenacted legislative proposals in the 112th Congress, E.O. 13636 mainly addresses two: information sharing and protection of privately held critical infrastructure. It does not provide exemptions from liability stemming from information sharing, which would require changes to current law. Several of the legislative proposals included such changes. With respect to protection of critical infrastructure, the provisions on designation of CI and identification of relevant regulations are related to those in some legislative proposals.

In the 113th Congress, some bills would provide explicit statutory authority for information-sharing along the lines of some bills in the 112th Congress. Others would authorize activities on developing a cybersecurity framework similar to those in the executive order.

The issuance of E.O. 13636, as with many other executive orders, raises questions about whether the order exceeds the scope of the President's authority, in relation to the constitutional separation of powers and validly enacted legislation. While answers to those questions are complex, the executive order specifies that implementation will be consistent with applicable law and that nothing in the order provides regulatory authority to an agency beyond that under existing law.

Overall, response to the executive order has been optimistic. Given the absence of comprehensive cybersecurity legislation, some security observers contend that the order is a necessary step in securing vital assets against cyberthreats. Others have argued, in contrast, that it offers little more than do existing processes, that it could make enactment of a bill less likely, or that it could lead to government intrusiveness into private-sector activities, for example through increased regulation under existing statutory authority. Despite considerable progress in meeting the specific objectives in the executive order, especially the NIST Framework, it still appears to be too early in the implementation of the order to determine whether such concerns will be addressed to the satisfaction of critics and skeptics.

The federal legislative framework for cybersecurity is complex, with more than 50 statutes addressing various aspects of it either directly or indirectly. Many observers have expressed doubt that the current statutory framework is sufficient to address the growing concerns about the security of cyberspace in the United States, especially with respect to critical infrastructure (CI).[1] Several legislative proposals were made in recent Congresses to address those concerns. While a few cybersecurity bills were enacted in the 113th Congress, they addressed only the security of federal information systems (S. 2521) and workforce issues (H.R. 2952 and S. 1691) and information-sharing activities (S. 2519) at the Department of Homeland Security (DHS).

Within the executive branch, both the George W. Bush and Obama Administrations have focused on improving the cybersecurity of critical infrastructure. The Bush Administration created the classified Comprehensive National Cybersecurity Initiative (the CNCI) in 2008.[2] The Obama Administration performed an interagency review of federal cybersecurity initiatives in 2009, culminating in the release of its *Cyberspace Policy Review*[3] and the creation of the White House position of Cybersecurity Coordinator. In the absence of enacted legislation, the Obama Administration began drafting a cybersecurity executive order in 2012. The development involved input from both federal agencies and stakeholders in the private sector.[4]

On February 12, 2013, President Obama issued Executive Order 13636, *Improving Critical Infrastructure Cybersecurity*,[5] along with Presidential Policy Directive 21 (PPD 21),[6] *Critical Infrastructure Security and Resilience.* The issuance of the executive order in the absence of congressional action raises several questions that are addressed in this report:

- What are the kinds of threats to the national security and economic interests of the United States that the executive order is intended to address?
- What steps does it take to address those threats, what is the status of their implementation, and what issues do they raise?
- What is the legislative and constitutional authority for the executive order?
- How do its provisions relate to those in legislative proposals in the 112th and 113th Congresses?

- What has been the reaction of stakeholders to the order and what issues does it raise?

Background: Threats and Consequences

> Repeated cyber intrusions into critical infrastructure demonstrate the need for improved cybersecurity. The cyber threat to critical infrastructure continues to grow and represents one of the most serious national security challenges we must confront. The national and economic security of the United States depends on the reliable functioning of the Nation's critical infrastructure in the face of such threats.[7]

Cyberthreats to U.S. infrastructure and other assets are a growing concern to policy makers. Information and communications technology (ICT)[8] is ubiquitous and relied upon for government services, corporate business processes, and individual professional and personal pursuits—almost every facet of modern life. Many ICT devices and other components are interdependent, and disruption of one component may have a negative, cascading effect on others. A denial of service, theft or manipulation of data, or damage to critical infrastructure through a cyber-based attack could have significant impacts on national security, the economy, and the livelihood and safety of individual citizens.

Cyberthreats

Cyber-based technologies[9] are now ubiquitous around the globe. The vast majority of users pursue lawful professional and personal objectives. However, criminals, terrorists, and spies also rely heavily on cyber-based technologies to support their objectives. These malefactors may access cyber-based technologies in order to deny service, steal or manipulate data, or use a device to launch an attack against itself or another piece of equipment. Entities using cyber-based technologies for illegal purposes take many forms and pursue a variety of actions counter to U.S. global security and economic interests. While E.O. 13636 discusses in general terms cyber-based threats directed at the nation's critical infrastructure, it does not identify the types of cyber-actors and possible consequences of a successful attack. Commonly recognized cyber-aggressors discussed below, along with representative examples of the harm they can inflict, include cyberterrorists, cyberspies, cyberthieves, cyberwarriors, and cyberhacktivists.

Cyberterrorists

Cyberterrorists are state-sponsored and non-state actors who engage in cyberattacks as a form of warfare. Transnational terrorist organizations, insurgents, and jihadists have used the Internet as a tool for planning attacks, radicalization and recruitment, a method of propaganda distribution, and a means of communication.[10] While no unclassified reports have been published regarding a terrorist-initiated cyberattack on U.S. critical infrastructure (CI),[11] the vulnerability of essential components of that infrastructure to access and even destruction via the Internet has been demonstrated. In 2009, the Department of Homeland Security (DHS) conducted an experiment that revealed some of the vulnerabilities to the nation's control systems that manage power generators and grids. The experiment, known as the Aurora Project, entailed a computer-based attack on a power generator's control system that caused operations to cease and the equipment to be destroyed.[12]

Cyberspies

Cyberspies are individuals who steal classified or proprietary information used by governments or private corporations to gain a competitive strategic, security, financial, or political advantage. These individuals often work at the behest of, and take direction from, foreign government entities. For example, a 2011 FBI report noted, "a company was the victim of an intrusion and had lost 10 years' worth of research and development data—valued at $1 billion—virtually overnight."[13] Likewise, in 2008 the Department of Defense's (DOD's) classified computer network system was unlawfully accessed and "the computer code, placed there by a foreign intelligence agency, uploaded itself undetected onto both classified and unclassified systems from which data could be transferred to servers under foreign control."[14] The U.S. intelligence community recently completed a classified National Intelligence Estimate (NIE) focused on cyberspying against U.S. targets. Reportedly, the NIE "concluded that the United States is the target of a massive, sustained cyber-espionage campaign that is threatening the country's economic competitiveness."[15] Media reports suggest that the NIE also assessed that Russia, Israel, and France also engage in illegal accessing of United States entities for economic intelligence purposes but notes that "cyber-espionage by those countries pales in comparison with China's effort."[16] A February 2013 report of an investigation by a private-sector security firm of intrusions against more than 100 targets over the past seven years states that the attacks were performed by a single Chinese group that appears to be linked to the People's Liberation Army.[17]

Cyberthieves

Cyberthieves are individuals who engage in illegal cyberattacks for monetary gain. Examples include an organization or individual who illegally accesses a technology system to steal and use or sell credit card numbers and someone who deceives a victim into providing access to a financial account. Cybercrime is widely regarded as lucrative and relatively low-risk for criminals and costly for victims, with some estimates placing the annual global cost to individuals as high as hundreds of billions of dollars.[18] However, making accurate estimates of such aggregate costs is problematic, and there does not appear to be any publicly available, comprehensive, reliable assessment of the overall costs of cyberattacks.

Cyberwarriors

Cyberwarriors are agents or quasi-agents of nation-states who develop capabilities and undertake cyberattacks in support of a country's strategic objectives.[19] These entities may or may not be acting on behalf of the government with respect to target selection, timing of the attack, and type(s) of cyberattack and are often blamed by the host country when accusations are levied by the nation that has been attacked. Often, when a foreign government is provided evidence that a cyberattack is emanating from its country, the nation that has been attacked is informed that the perpetrators acted of their own volition and not at the behest of the government. In August 2012 a series of cyberattacks were directed against Saudi Aramco, the world's largest oil and gas producer and most valuable company. The attacks compromised 30,000 of the company's computers and the code was apparently designed to disrupt or halt the production oil. Some security officials have suggested that

Iran may have supported this attack.[20] However, other observers suggest that the perpetrator of the attack was an employee of Saudi Aramco.[21]

Cyberhacktivists

Cyberhacktivists are individuals who perform cyberattacks for pleasure, or for philosophical or other nonmonetary reasons. Examples include someone who attacks a technology system as a personal challenge (who might be termed a "classic" hacker), and a "hacktivist" such as a member of the cyber-group Anonymous who undertakes an attack for political reasons. The activities of these groups can range from simple nuisance-related denial of service attacks to disrupting government and private corporation business processes.

Cyberthreats and Implications for U.S. Policy

These different kinds of cyber-aggressors and the types of attacks they can pursue are not mutually exclusive. For example, a hacker targeting the intellectual property of a corporation may be categorized as both a cyberthief and a cyberspy, and possibly a cyberwarrior if the activity is conducted by a military enterprise, as has been claimed for some such attacks.[22] A cyberterrorist and cyberwarrior may be employing different technological capabilities in support of a nation's security and political objectives. Ascertaining information about the aggressor and its capabilities and intentions is very difficult.[23] The threats posed by these aggressors, coupled with the United States' proclivity to be an early adopter of emerging technologies,[24] which often contain unrecognized vulnerabilities and are introduced into existing computer networks, make for a complex environment when considering operational responses, policies, and legislation designed to safeguard the nation's strategic economic and security interests. E.O. 13636 discusses the nation's reliance on cyber-based technologies and identifies activities and reporting requirements to be addressed by numerous federal government departments and agencies.

OVERVIEW OF THE EXECUTIVE ORDER

The federal role in what is now called cybersecurity[25] has been debated for more than a decade. Much of the recent debate has focused on two issues: sharing of cybersecurity-related information within and across sectors, and the cybersecurity of CI sectors, including federal systems. E.O. 13636 attempts to address both of those issues, as well as others.

It uses existing statutory and constitutional authority to

- *expand information sharing and collaboration* between the government and the private sector, including sharing classified information by broadening a program developed for the defense industrial base to other CI sectors;
- *develop a voluntary framework of cybersecurity standards and best practices* for protecting CI, through a public/private effort;
- *establish a consultative process* for improving CI cybersecurity;
- *identify CI with especially high priority for protection,* using the consultative process;
- *establish a program with incentives for voluntary adoption of the framework* by CI owners and operators;
- *review cybersecurity regulatory requirements* to determine if they are sufficient and appropriate; and
- *incorporate privacy and civil liberties protections* in activities under the order.

The information-sharing and framework provisions in particular have received significant public attention.

Information Sharing

Improved sharing of information on cybersecurity threats, vulnerabilities, attacks, prevention, and response both within and across sectors, including government, is thought by most experts to be critical to improving cybersecurity but fraught with barriers and uncertainties, relating especially to privacy, liability, reputation costs,[26] protection of proprietary information, antitrust law, and misuse of shared information. A few sectors are subject to federal notification requirements,[27] but most such information sharing is voluntary, often through sector-specific Information Sharing and Analysis Centers (ISACs)[28] or programs under the auspices of the Department of Homeland Security (DHS) or sector-specific agencies.[29] A key question is how to balance the need for better, more timely cybersecurity information with other needs such as protection of privacy and civil rights as well as legitimate business and economic interests.

To improve information sharing, the order builds on a voluntary effort established in May 2011. That program, known as the DIB[30] Cyber Pilot, involved several defense industry partners, the National Security Agency (NSA), and DOD[31] in sharing classified threat-vector information among stakeholders. One aspect was sharing by the NSA of threat signatures obtained through its computer monitoring activities.[32]

In May 2012, DOD established the DIB Cybersecurity/Information Assurance (CS/IA) Program,[33] making it broadly available to all eligible DIB partners. Under the program, DOD provides defense contractors with classified and unclassified cyberthreat information and cybersecurity best practices, while DIB participants report cyber-incidents, coordinate on mitigation strategies, and participate in cyber intrusion damage assessments if DOD information is compromised. Participating companies may also join an optional classified-information sharing subprogram, known as the DIB Cybersecurity Enhancement Program (DECS)—the former DIB Cyber Pilot[34]—by meeting specified security requirements.

To expand the program beyond the DIB sector, DHS established the Joint Cybersecurity Services Pilot (JCSP) in January 2012, the first phase of which focused on the DECS program and shifted operational relationships with participating commercial service providers (CSPs) to DHS. DHS made the program permanent in July 2012. In January 2013, the department named the program Enhanced Cybersecurity Services (ECS) and expanded it to all CI sectors, including the federal sector,[35] as well as nonfederal government entities.[36] In this program, DHS does not share threat indicators with CI entities directly but rather with participating CSPs (see *Figure 1*). DOD still serves as the point of contact for participating DIB contractors.[37]

The executive order builds on such established programs by requiring the Secretary of Homeland Security to

- expand ECS to all CI sectors;
- expedite processing of security clearances to appropriate CI personnel; and

- expand programs to place relevant private-sector experts in federal agencies on a temporary basis.

It also requires the Secretary of Homeland Security and the Attorney General to expedite collection of threat indicators and dissemination of them to targeted entities.

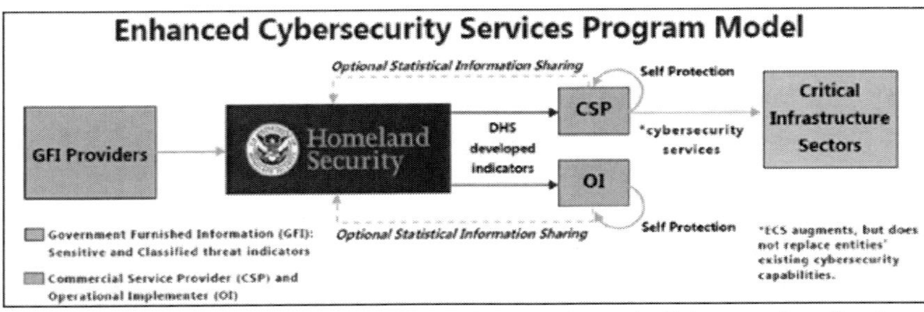

Source: Department of Homeland Security, "Enhanced Cybersecurity Services," November 14, 2014, http://www.dhs.gov/sites/default/files/publications/ECS-Fact-Sheet.pdf.

Figure 1. Schematic Description of ECS Information-Sharing Process.

Voluntary Cybersecurity Framework

The increasing potential for attacks that might cripple components of CI or otherwise damage the national economy, as discussed above, has led to debate about the best ways to protect those sectors beyond improvements in information sharing. Some CI sectors are subject to federal regulation with respect to cybersecurity,[38] while the protection of others relies largely on voluntary efforts. The efficacy of that mix of voluntary and regulatory efforts has been a prominent issue in the ongoing debate about federal cybersecurity legislation. Proponents of additional regulation argue that the voluntary approach has not provided sufficient protection and that regulation has been effective in sectors such as electricity and financial services. Opponents argue that expanding federal requirements would be costly and ineffective and may impede innovation. Also, there has appeared to be some uncertainty about the extent to which existing statutory authority would permit new cybersecurity requirements in some sectors.

E.O. 13636 builds on the involvement of the National Institute of Standards and Technology (NIST) in the development of cybersecurity technical standards[39] and its statutory responsibilities to work with both government and private entities on various aspects of standards and technology.[40] The order requires the following:

- *NIST*—lead the development of the Cybersecurity Framework, an effort that uses an open, consultative process to reduce cybersecurity risks to CI; focuses on cross-sector, voluntary consensus standards and business best practices; is technology-neutral; identifies areas for improvement; and is reviewed and updated as necessary.
- *Secretary of Homeland Security*—set performance goals for the framework, establish a voluntary program to support its adoption, and coordinate establishment of incentives for adoption.
- *Sector-specific agencies*—coordinate review of the framework and development of sector-specific guidance, and report annually to the President on participation by CI sectors.
- *CI regulatory agencies*—engage in consultative review of the framework, determine whether existing cybersecurity requirements are adequate, and report to the President whether the agencies have authority to establish requirements that sufficiently address the risks (it does not state that the agencies must establish such requirements, however), propose additional authority where required, and identify and recommend remedies for ineffective, conflicting, or excessively burdensome cybersecurity requirements.

The executive order stipulates that it provides no authority for regulating critical infrastructure in addition to that under existing law, and it does not alter existing authority.

The development of the framework is arguably the most innovative and labor-intensive requirement in the executive order. None of the major legislative proposals in the 111th and 112th Congresses had proposed using NIST to coordinate an effort led by the private sector to develop a framework for cybersecurity, such as was envisioned by the executive order. Hundreds of entities have been involved in NIST's efforts, which led to release of the first version of the framework in February 2014.[41]

The framework is intended to provide broad guidance on cybersecurity using a risk-based approach that can be adapted to the needs of different CI sectors. It consists of three parts:

- The *core* is a common set of activities and outcomes applicable to all CI sectors It is organized into five functions—*identify, protect, detect, respond,* and *recover*—that are widely recognized components of any cybersecurity management lifecycle, along with associated programmatic and technical outcomes, for example, "access control" and "data-at-rest is protected."[42]
- The *profile* describes an entity's current and target cybersecurity postures, based on business needs identified by considering the relevant *core* components. It can be used to support prioritization of action and measurement of progress. The current profile lists outcomes that are being achieved, while the target profile lists the outcomes needed to achieve desired cybersecurity goals.
- The *implementation tiers* characterize an entity's current and intended practices, which can range from "informal, reactive responses" (Tier 1) to "agile and risk-informed" approaches (Tier 4).[43]

The framework is not intended to be static but will be updated as required. Areas that NIST has already identified for improvement include authentication, automated sharing of indicators, assessment of the degree of conformity to risk-management requirements, cybersecurity workforce needs, data analytics, supply-chain risk management, technical standards relating to privacy, alignment of the framework with federal agency cybersecurity requirements, and international aspects and implications.[44] Several of those are broadly recognized as key issues in cybersecurity.

To assist in adoption and implementation of the framework by CI entities, DHS has developed the Critical Infrastructure Cyber Community C^3 Voluntary Program. Its goals are to help CI entities understand and use the framework and obtain feedback from them on improvements.[45]

Other Provisions

The executive order contains several additional provisions on CI cybersecurity:

Acquisition and Contracting. The Secretary of Defense and the Administrator of General Services must make recommendations to the President on incorporating security standards in acquisition and contracting processes, including harmonization of cybersecurity requirements.

Consultative Process. The Secretary of Homeland Security is required to establish a broad consultative process to coordinate improvements in the cybersecurity of critical infrastructure.

Cybersecurity Workforce. The Secretary of Homeland Security is required to coordinate technical assistance to critical-infrastructure regulatory agencies on development of their cybersecurity workforce and programs.

High-Risk Critical Infrastructure. The order requires the Secretary of Homeland Security to use consistent and objective criteria, the consultative process established under the order, and information from relevant stakeholders to identify and update annually a list of critical infrastructure for which a cyberattack could have catastrophic regional or national impact, but not including commercial information technology products or consumer information technology services. The Secretary must confidentially notify owners and operators of critical infrastructure that is so identified of its designation and provide a process to request reconsideration.

Privacy and Civil Liberties. The order requires agencies to ensure incorporation of privacy and civil liberties protections in agency activities under the order, including protection from disclosure of information submitted by private entities, as permitted by law. The DHS Chief Privacy Officer and Officer for Civil Rights and Civil Liberties must assess risks to privacy and civil liberties of DHS activities under the order and recommend methods of mitigation to the Secretary in a public report. Agency privacy and civil liberties officials must provide assessments of agency activities to DHS.

E.O. 13636 Implementation Deliverables and Deadlines

The order contains several requirements with deadlines, and other requirements with no associated dates. In March 2013, DHS announced that it had formed a task force with eight working groups focused on the various deliverables for which it is responsible.[46] Several deliverables have specific associated dates:

June 12, 2013

- Instructions for producing unclassified threat reports (Secretary of Homeland Security, Attorney General, Director of National Intelligence) (Sec. 4(a)).

- Procedures for expansion of the Enhanced Cybersecurity Services Program (Secretary of Homeland Security) (Sec. 4(c)).[47]
- Recommendations to the President on incentives to participate in the framework (Secretaries of Homeland Security, Commerce, and the Treasury) (Sec. 8(d)).[48]
- Recommendations to the President on acquisitions and contracts (Secretary of Defense, Administrator of General Services) (Sec. 8(e)).[49]

July 12, 2013

- Designation of critical infrastructure at greatest risk (Secretary of Homeland Security) (Sec. 9(a)).[50]

October 10, 2013

- Publication of preliminary Cybersecurity Framework (Director of the National Institute of Standards and Technology) (Sec. 7(e)).[51]

February 12, 2014

- Report on privacy and civil liberties, preceded by consultations (Chief Privacy Officer and Officer for Civil Rights and Civil Liberties of DHS) (Sec. 5(b)).[52]
- Publication of final Cybersecurity Framework (Director of the National Institute of Standards and Technology) (Sec. 7(e)).[53]

May 13, 2014

- Reports to the President on review of regulatory requirements (agencies with regulatory responsibilities for critical infrastructure) (Sec. 10(a)).[54]
- Proposed additional risk mitigation actions (agencies with regulatory responsibilities for critical infrastructure) (Sec. 10(b)).[55]

February 12, 2016

- Reports to the Office of Management and Budget on ineffective, conflicting, or burdensome requirements (agencies with regulatory responsibilities for critical infrastructure) (Sec. 10(c)).

The order also includes more than 20 actions for which no specific date is provided. Some of the deliverables have been made publicly available, largely in accordance with the deadlines in the order, as noted above in the footnotes. Some provisions appeared to have had some effect soon after the order was issued. For example, the provision on expedited security clearances was apparently used to facilitate communication by the FBI with banks in response to a cyberattack in the spring of 2013 on several banks.[56]

The assessments of regulatory requirements and proposed actions focused on three agencies: DHS, the Environmental Protection Agency (EPA), and the Department of Health and Human Services (HHS). The Administration concluded that "existing regulatory requirements, when complemented with strong voluntary partnerships, are capable of mitigating cyber risks to our critical systems and information."[57]

Relationship of the Executive Order to Presidential Policy Directive 21

Presidential Policy Directive 21 (PPD 21),[58] *Critical Infrastructure Security and Resilience,* on protection of critical infrastructure, was released in tandem with Executive Order 13636. PPD 21 supersedes Homeland Security Presidential Directive 7 (HSPD 7), *Critical Infrastructure Identification, Prioritization, and Protection,* released December 17, 2003. The PPD seeks to strengthen both the cyber- and physical security and resilience of critical infrastructure by

- clarifying functional relationships among federal agencies, including the establishment of separate DHS operational centers for physical and cyberinfrastructure;
- identifying baseline requirements for information sharing, to facilitate timely and efficient information exchange between government and critical-infrastructure entities while respecting privacy and civil liberties;
- applying integration and analysis capabilities in DHS to prioritize and manage risks and impacts, recommend preventive and responsive actions, and support incident management and restoration efforts for critical infrastructure; and
- organizing research and development (R&D) to enable secure and resilient critical infrastructure, enhance impact-modeling capabilities, and support strategic DHS guidance.

PPD 21 Implementation Deliverables and Deadlines

June 12, 2013

- Description of functional relationships within DHS and across other federal agencies relating to critical infrastructure security and resilience (Secretary of Homeland Security).[59]

July 12, 2013

- Analysis of public-private partnership models with recommended improvements (Secretary of Homeland Security).[60]

August 11, 2013

- Convening of experts to identify baseline information and intelligence exchange requirements (Secretary of Homeland Security).

October 10, 2013

- Demonstration of "near real-time" situational-awareness capability for critical infrastructure (Secretary of Homeland Security).
- Updated National Infrastructure Protection Plan that addresses implementation of the directive (Secretary of Homeland Security).[61]

February 12, 2015

- First quadrennial National Critical Infrastructure Security and Resilience R&D Plan (Secretary of Homeland Security).[62]

In addition to DHS, the directive describes specific responsibilities for the Departments of Commerce, Interior, Justice, and State, the Intelligence Community, the General Services Administration, the Federal Communications Commission, the sector-specific agencies, and all federal departments and agencies.[63]

SCOPE OF PRESIDENTIAL AUTHORITY

E.O. 13636 was issued in the wake of the lack of enactment of cybersecurity legislation in the 112th Congress, apparently at least in part as a response to that.[64] That raises questions about what authority the President has to act on this matter through an executive order. That issue is discussed below.

The issuance of an executive order frequently raises questions about whether the order exceeds the scope of the President's authority, in relation to the constitutional separation of powers and validly enacted legislation. Since the latter half of the 20th century, these questions have typically been evaluated using the tripartite framework set forth by U.S. Supreme Court Justice Jackson in his concurring opinion in the case of *Youngstown Sheet & Tube Company v. Sawyer*.[65] First, if the President has acted according to an express or implied grant of congressional authority, presidential "authority is at its maximum." Second, in situations where Congress has neither granted nor denied authority to the President, the President acts in reliance only "upon his own independent powers, but there is a zone of twilight in which he and Congress may have concurrent authority, or in which its distribution is uncertain." Third, in instances where presidential action is "incompatible with the express or implied will of Congress," the power of the President is at its minimum. In such a circumstance, presidential action must rest upon an exclusive Article II power.

As an example of the first category, Congress has previously provided explicit statutory authority for the executive to regulate the security of private entities.[66] For example,[67] chemical facilities are subject to chemical facility anti-terrorism standards (CFATS) promulgated by the Department of Homeland Security (DHS), which include provisions requiring chemical facilities to take measures to protect against cyberthreats.[68] Similarly, the Maritime Transportation Security Act (MTSA) gives the Coast Guard the authority to regulate the security of maritime facilities and vessels, including requiring security plans that contain provisions for the security of communications systems used in those facilities.[69] In these and other situations where Congress has provided explicit regulatory authority to the executive branch related to cybersecurity, the President's authority to direct sector-specific agencies to coordinate, evaluate, develop, or implement appropriate cybersecurity standards pursuant to the executive order[70] would appear to be at its maximum.

In other cases, where there may only be congressional silence regarding the President's authority to direct action on cybersecurity issues, an argument could be made that the issuance of such an executive order falls within the "zone of twilight," assuming that the action could be concurrently justified under some explicit or implied power granted to the President by the Constitution. For example, Section 9 of E.O. 13636 directs the Secretary of Homeland Security to use a risk-based approach to identify critical infrastructure where a cybersecurity incident could result in catastrophic effects.[71] While such identification is arguably authorized under the Homeland

Security Act of 2002,[72] it might alternatively be justified under the President's constitutional authority to request written opinions from the heads of executive departments.[73]

However, some past legislative proposals may be beyond the reach of unilateral executive action. For example, prior proposals to regulate the cybersecurity of critical infrastructure have also proposed limits on liability or safe harbors for regulated entities that comply with the regulatory schemes,[74] because the creation of a regulatory scheme can have an adverse effect on the exposure of regulated entities to civil liability.[75] The scope of such proposed limits has ranged from complete immunity, to lesser restrictions such as prohibitions against the awarding of punitive damages. Such limits on liability may also be made dependent upon an entity's satisfaction of its regulatory obligations, in order to create a further incentive for compliance.

The abrogation of civil claims under common law or contract law without explicit congressional authorization may be difficult to justify on the executive's constitutional powers alone. Notably, the executive order does not purport to provide any similar liability safe harbors for private entities that comply with cybersecurity standards developed pursuant to the executive order. While it does direct the Secretary of Homeland Security to coordinate the establishment of a set of incentives to promote voluntary participation in the critical infrastructure program, it also acknowledges that some incentives may require legislation affirmatively authorizing such limitations.[76] This is not to say that the executive order will have no impact on liability. The publication of recommendations or risk assessments, as provided under the executive order, may be used by litigants as evidence of the appropriate standard of care to apply in tort litigation resulting from a cybersecurity incident, even if such standards are not controlling.[77]

Similarly, it may not be possible for an executive order to authorize telecommunications providers to engage in more aggressive monitoring of communications networks to help identify cyber threats or attacks in real-time. Such an executive action would contravene current federal laws protecting electronic communications, and would be evaluated in the third category of Justice Jackson's *Youngstown* framework, where the President's power is at its minimum. Such an executive order would not be effective, unless such action fell within a power exclusively granted to the executive by the Constitution. Consistent with this analysis, E.O. 13636 does not purport to provide any authority for private telecommunications providers to engage in monitoring of their networks.

RELATIONSHIP TO LEGISLATIVE PROPOSALS

While E.O. 13636 does not purport to create new authorities, there are commonalities between some of its provisions and some of the cybersecurity proposals from the 112th and 113th Congresses. A comparison of a selection of the issues covered by those proposals and the executive order is below.[78]

Several comprehensive legislative proposals on cybersecurity in the 112th Congress received considerable attention, including a Senate bill, a set of bill proposals by the Obama Administration, and a report with recommendations from a House Republican task force,[79] which informed several House bills. The various proposals differed both in some of the issues they addressed and in how they approached them. Among the issues addressed were the following:

- Cybersecurity workforce authorities and programs,
- Cybersecurity R&D,
- Data-breach notification,
- DHS authorities for protection of federal systems,
- FISMA reform,
- Information sharing,
- Penalties for cybercrime,
- Protection of privately held CI, including public/private sector collaboration and regulation of privately held CI,
- Public awareness about cybersecurity, and
- Supply-chain vulnerabilities.

E.O. 13636 mainly addresses two of those topics: information sharing and protection of privately held CI. With respect to information sharing, the executive order does not provide exemptions from liability stemming from information sharing, which would require changes to current law. Several of the legislative proposals included such changes. Also, some proposals included the creation of new entities for information sharing, whereas the executive order uses existing mechanisms.

With respect to protection of critical infrastructure, the provisions on designation of CI and identification of relevant regulations are related to those in some legislative proposals in the 112th Congress. The role of NIST in developing the Cybersecurity Framework was not in the legislative proposals from that Congress, although several would have expanded the agency's role in cybersecurity.

In the 113th Congress, H.R. 624 and S. 2588 would address information sharing, and H.R. 3696 and S. 1353 would require NIST to lead a public/private effort similar to the process by which the Cybersecurity Framework is being developed. Both House bills passed in the House, H.R. 694 in April 2013 and H.R. 3696 in July 2014, but some provisions in each were controversial.[80]

Reactions to the Executive Order

Given the absence of enacted comprehensive cybersecurity legislation, some security observers have contended that the executive order is a necessary step in securing vital assets against cyberthreats. Proponents of the framework point to its ability to alleviate the problems created by a lack of understanding about cybersecurity issues and practices among different classes of stakeholders. They claim that the framework provides a common, nontechnical basis for developing consensus on how best to approach cybersecurity needs.[81]

Other observers, however, have raised concerns.[82] Common themes by such critics have included the following claims:

- *The order offers little more than do existing processes.* Such critics point out that, for example, the Enhanced Cybersecurity Services program was in place before the release of the order, and that a variety of efforts have been underway to develop and adopt voluntary standards and best practices in cybersecurity for many years. Proponents of the order argue that it lays out and clarifies Obama Administration goals, requires specific deliverables and timelines, and that the framework and other provisions are in fact new with the executive order.
- *The order could make enactment of legislation less likely.* These critics express concern that Congress might decide to wait until the major provisions of the order have been fully implemented before considering legislation. Proponents state that immediate action was necessary in the absence of legislation, and that changes in current law are necessary no matter how successful the executive order might be, to provide liability protections for information sharing and to meet other needs.

- *The process for developing the framework is either too slow or too rushed.* Some observers believe that some actions to protect critical infrastructure are well-established and should be taken immediately, given the nature and extent of the current threat. They state that the year-long process to develop the framework may have delayed implementation of needed security measures,[83] creating unnecessary and unacceptable risks. Others counter that widespread adoption of the framework requires consensus, which takes time to achieve, and that the one-year timeframe may be insufficient, given that the process for developing and updating consensus standards often takes several years. In fact, some CI entities have reportedly delayed implementation while waiting for additional federal guidance.[84] Some also state that the framework process does not preclude entities from adopting established security measures immediately.
- The framework risks becoming a form of de facto regulation, or alternatively, its voluntary nature makes it insufficiently enforceable. Another concern of some is that the executive order could lead to government intrusiveness into private-sector activities, for example through increased regulation under existing statutory authority,[85] while others contend that voluntary measures have a poor history of success. Some others, however, have argued that changes in the business environment—such as the advent of continuous monitoring, more powerful analytical tools, and a better prepared workforce—improve the likelihood that a voluntary approach can be successful.[86]
- The order could lead to overclassification or underclassification of high-risk critical infrastructure by DHS. Some observers have expressed concern that the requirement in the order for DHS to designate high-risk critical infrastructure may be insufficiently clear and could lead to either harmfully expansive designations or inappropriate exclusions of entities.[87] This might be particularly a problem if the criteria are not sufficiently validated.[88]

It appears to be too early in the implementation of the executive order to determine how effectively the concerns described above will be addressed and whether the responses will satisfy critics and skeptics. Overall, however, response to the order from the private sector—including critical-infrastructure entities, trade associations, and cybersecurity practitioners—appears to be largely positive. Some organizations and experts have urged adoption of the framework by CI entities.[89]

In August 2014, NIST requested public comments on implementation of the framework and posted more than 60 it received from various companies, trade associations, and other organizations.[90] The responses demonstrate a range of understanding and implementation both across and within sectors and generally support the contention that additional experience will be necessary before the success of the framework at improving CI cybersecurity can be adequately assessed.

End Notes

[1] CI is defined in 42 U.S.C. §5195c(e) as "systems and assets, whether physical or virtual, so vital to the United States that the incapacity or destruction of such systems and assets would have a debilitating impact on security, national economic security, national public health or safety, or any combination of those matters." For more information on critical infrastructure, see CRS Report RL30153, Critical Infrastructures: Background, Policy, and Implementation, by John D. Moteff,. For a discussion of the legislative framework for cybersecurity, see CRS Report R42114, Federal Laws Relating to Cybersecurity: Overview of Major Issues, Current Laws, and Proposed Legislation, by Eric A. Fischer.

[2] National Security Presidential Directive 54 / Homeland Security Presidential Directive 23 (NSPD-54/HSPD-23).

[3] The White House, Cyberspace Policy Review, May 29, 2009, http://www.whitehouse.gov/ assets/documents/ Cyberspace_Policy_Review_final.pdf; The White House, "Cyberspace Policy Review [Supporting Documents]," May 2009, http://www.whitehouse.gov/ cyberreview/documents/.

[4] Tony Romm, "White House Moves on Cybersecurity," Politico, November 27, 2012, http://www.politico.com/news/ stories/1112/84247.html.

[5] Executive Order 13636, "Improving Critical Infrastructure Cybersecurity," Federal Register 78, no. 33 (February 19, 2013): 11737–11744. The information in this report is derived from unclassified sources, including this Executive Order, and does not reflect information that may be included in a classified Presidential Order or other classified documents addressing cyberthreats to the United States.

[6] The White House, "Critical Infrastructure Security and Resilience," Presidential Policy Directive 21, (February 12, 2013), http://www.whitehouse.gov/the-press-office/2013/02/12/ presidential-policy-directive-critical-infrastructuresecurity-and-resil.

[7] E.O. 13636.

[8] The term ICT is increasingly used instead of IT (information technologies) because of the convergence of telecommunications and computer technology. However, the current federal legislative framework for cybersecurity does not reflect that convergence and generally treats IT and telecommunications as separate technologies.

[9] For purposes of this report, cyber-based technologies means electronic devices that access or rely on the transfer of bytes of data to perform a mechanical function. The devices can access cyberspace (including the Internet) through the use of physical connections or wireless signals.

[10] For additional background information, see archived CRS Report RL33123, Terrorist Capabilities for Cyberattack: Overview and Policy Issues, by John W. Rollins and Clay Wilson.

[11] The Executive Order uses the same definition of critical infrastructure as 42 U.S.C. 5195c(e): "systems and assets, whether physical or virtual, so vital to the United States that the incapacity or destruction of such systems and assets would have a debilitating impact on security, national economic security, national public health or safety, or any combination of those matters."

[12] See "Challenges Remain in DHS' Efforts to Secure Control Systems," Department of Homeland Security, Office of Inspector General, August 2009. For a discussion of how computer code may have caused the halting of operations at an Iranian nuclear facility see CRS Report R41524, The Stuxnet Computer Worm: Harbinger of an Emerging Warfare Capability, by Paul K. Kerr, John W. Rollins, and Catherine A. Theohary.

[13] Executive Assistant Director Shawn Henry, "Responding to the Cyber Threat," Federal Bureau of Investigation, Baltimore, MD, 2011.

[14] Department of Defense Deputy Secretary of Defense William J. Lynn III, "Defending a New Domain," Foreign Affairs, October 2010.

[15] Ellen Nakashima, "U.S. Said to Be Target of Massive Cyber-Espionage Campaign," Washington Post, February 10, 2013.

[16] Ibid.

[17] Mandiant, APT1: Exposing One of China's Cyber Espionage Units, February 18, 2013, http://intelreport.mandiant.com/Mandiant_APT1_Report.pdf.

[18] For discussions of federal law and issues relating to cybercrime, see CRS Report 97-1025, Cybercrime: An Overview of the Federal Computer Fraud and Abuse Statute and Related Federal Criminal Laws, by Charles Doyle; and CRS Report R41927, The Interplay of Borders, Turf, Cyberspace, and Jurisdiction: Issues Confronting U.S. Law Enforcement, by Kristin Finklea.

[19] For additional information, see CRS Report RL31787, Information Operations, Cyberwarfare, and Cybersecurity: Capabilities and Related Policy Issues, by Catherine A. Theohary.

[20] Wael Mahdi, "Saudi Arabia Says Aramco Cyberattack Came from Foreign States," Bloomberg News, December 9, 2012, http://www.bloomberg.com/news/2012-12-09/saudi-arabia-says-aramco-cyberattack-came-from-foreignstates.html.

[21] Michael Riley and Eric Engleman, "Code in Aramco Cyber Attack Indicates Lone Perpetrator," Bloomberg Businessweek, October 25, 2012.

[22] Mandiant, APT1: Exposing One of China's Cyber Espionage Units, op. cit.

[23] The concept of attribution in the cybersecurity context entails an attempt to identify with some degree of specificity and confidence the geographic location, identity, capabilities, and intention of the cyber-aggressor. Mobile technologies and sophisticated data routing processes and techniques often make attribution difficult for U.S. intelligence and law enforcement communities.

[24] Emerging cyber-based technologies that may be vulnerable to the actions of a cyber-aggressor include items that are in use but not yet widely adopted or are currently being developed. For additional information on how the convergence of inexpensive, highly sophisticated, and easily accessible technology is providing opportunities for cyber-aggressors to exploit vulnerabilities found in a technologically laden society see Office of the Director of National Intelligence, "Global Trends 2030," 2013, http://www.dni.gov/index.php/about/organization/global-trends-2030.

[25] Cybersecurity is a convenient umbrella term that tends to defy precise consensus definition. Several different terms are in use that have related meanings. For example, information security is defined in some subsections of federal copyright law to mean "activities carried out in order to identify and address the vulnerabilities of a government computer, computer system, or computer network" (17 U.S.C. 1201(e), 1202(d)), and, in the Federal Information Security Management Act (FISMA, 44 U.S.C. 3542) as "protecting information and information systems from unauthorized access, use, disclosure, disruption, modification, or destruction" to provide integrity, confidentiality, and availability of the information. Other terms often used include information assurance, computer security, and network security.

[26] Reputation costs refers to the various forms of economic and other harm that an entity may experience as a result of damage to its reputation with customers or others. For example, if a company experiences a cyberattack in which its customer records are stolen or compromised, and the attack is made public, customers may switch to other companies for which attacks have not been made public, whether or not they have occurred.

[27] Notable examples include the chemical industry, electricity, financial, and transportation sectors.

[28] See, e.g., ISAC Council, "National Council of ISACS," 2014, http://www.isaccouncil.org/.

[29] See, e.g., Department of Homeland Security, "Critical Infrastructure Protection Partnerships and Information Sharing," 2013, http://www.dhs.gov/critical-infrastructure-protection-partnerships-and-information-sharing.

[30] DIB refers to the Defense Industrial Base, one of the CI sectors identified by DHS.

[31] NSA is a DOD-led agency but has some government-wide responsibilities as a member of the intelligence community.

[32] The program may in some ways be considered a private-sector version of DHS's EINSTEIN 3 cybersecurity initiative for federal systems (see, for example, Department of Homeland Security, Privacy Impact Assessment for the Enhanced Cybersecurity Services (ECS), January 16, 2013, http://www.dhs.gov/sites/default/files/publications/privacy/ privacy_pia_nppd_ecs_jan2013.pdf).

[33] 32 C.F.R. Part 236.

[34] John Reed, "DoD-DHS' Info Sharing Program on Cyber Threats Isn't Shrinking (Updated)," Foreign Policy: Killer Apps, October 9, 2012, http://killerapps.foreignpolicy.com/posts/2012/10/09/ dod_dhs_cyber_threat_info_sharing_program_isnt_shrinking.

[35] Department of Homeland Security, Privacy Impact Assessment for ECS.

[36] Department of Homeland Security, "Enhanced Cybersecurity Services," September 8, 2014, http://www.dhs.gov/ enhanced-cybersecurity-services.

[37] Ibid.

[38] For discussion of regulations on security of information systems for some CI sectors, see Government Accountability Office, Information Technology: Federal Laws, Regulations, and Mandatory Standards for Securing Private Sector Information Technology Systems and Data in Critical Infrastructure Sectors, GAO-08-1075R, September 16, 2008, http://www.gao.gov/assets/100/95747.pdf.

[39] See, e.g., National Institute of Standards and Technology, "Computer Security Resource Center," December 8, 2014, http://csrc.nist.gov/.

[40] 15 U.S.C. §272.

[41] National Institute of Standards and Technology, "Cybersecurity Framework," August 26, 2014, http://www.nist.gov/cyberframework/index.cfm.

[42] National Institute of Standards and Technology, Framework for Improving Critical Infrastructure Cybersecurity, Version 1.0, February 12, 2014, http://www.nist.gov/cyber

framework/upload/cybersecurity-framework-021214- final.pdf. The core also includes relevant references, such as publications by NIST and other organizations, for each outcome.

[43] Ibid.

[44] National Institute of Standards and Technology, "NIST Roadmap for Improving Critical Infrastructure Cybersecurity," February 12, 2014, http://www.nist.gov/cyberframework/upload/roadmap-021214.pdf.

[45] Department of Homeland Security, "About the Critical Infrastructure Cyber Community C3 Voluntary Program," May 21, 2014, http://www.dhs.gov/about-critical-infrastructure-cyber-community-c%C2%B3-voluntary-program.

[46] Department of Homeland Security, "Integrated Task Force," March 18, 2013, http://www.dhs.gov/sites/default/files/publications/EO-PPD%20Fact%20Sheet%2018 March13.pdf.

[47] Department of Homeland Security, "Enhanced Cybersecurity Services."

[48] Department of Homeland Security Integrated Task Force, Executive Order 13636: Improving Critical Infrastructure Cybersecurity: Incentives Study Analytic Report, June 12, 2013, http://www.dhs.gov/sites/default/files/publications/ dhs-eo13636-analytic-report-cybersecurity-incentives-study.pdf; Department of Commerce, Recommendations to the President on Incentives for Critical Infrastructure Owners and Operators to Join a Voluntary Cybersecurity Program, August 6, 2013, http://www.ntia.doc.gov/files/ntia/ Commerce_Incentives_Recommendations_Final.pdf; Department of the Treasury, Summary Report to the President on Cybersecurity Incentives Pursuant to Executive Order 13636, August 6, 2013, http://www.treasury.gov/press-center/Documents/Treasury%20Report%20 (Summary)%20to%20the%20President%20on%20Cybersecurity%20Incentives_FINAL.pdf.

[49] Department of Defense and General Services Administration, Improving Cybersecurity and Resilience through Acquisition, November 2013, http://www.gsa.gov/portal/mediaId/185367/fileName/IMPROVING_CYBERSECURITY_AND_RESILIENCE_THROUGH_ACQUISITION.action.

[50] See Statement of Robert Kolasky, Department of Homeland Security, Oversight of Executive Order 13636 and Development of the Cybersecurity Framework, Before the House Committee on Homeland Security, Subcommittee on Cybersecurity, Infrastructure Protection, and Security Technologies, July 18, 2013, http://docs.house.gov/meetings/HM/HM08/20130718/101151/HHRG-113-HM08-Wstate-KolaskyR-20130718.pdf.

[51] National Institute of Standards and Technology, Preliminary Cybersecurity Framework, October 22, 2013, http://www.nist.gov/itl/upload/preliminary-cybersecurity-framework.pdf.

[52] Department of Homeland Security, The Privacy Office and the Office for Civil Rights and Civil Liberties, Executive Order 13636: Privacy and Civil Liberties Assessment Report, April 2014, http://www.dhs.gov/sites/default/files/ publications/2014-privacy-and-civil-liberties-assessment-report.pdf.

[53] National Institute of Standards and Technology, "Cybersecurity Framework."

[54] Michael Daniel, "Assessing Cybersecurity Regulations," The White House Blog, May 22, 2014, http://www.whitehouse.gov/blog/2014/05/22/assessing-cybersecurity-regulations.

[55] Ibid.

[56] Joseph Menn, "FBI Says More Cooperation with Banks Key to Probe of Cyber Attacks," Reuters, May 13, 2013, http://www.reuters.com/article/2013/05/13/us-cyber-summit-fbi-banks-idUSBRE94C0XH20130513.

[57] Daniel, "Assessing Cybersecurity Regulations." The document notes that the executive order does not apply to independent regulatory agencies.

[58] The White House, "PPD 21."

[59] Department of Homeland Security Integrated Task Force, "National Infrastructure Protection Plan Update – Public Slides for National Infrastructure Advisory Council," July 17, 2013, http://www.dhs.gov/sites/default/files/publications/final-niac-brief-2013-07-11-v2-expan ded. pdf.

[60] Ibid.

[61] This document was not released on October 10, with a draft version reportedly criticized by industry representatives (see Jason Miller, "Industry, DHS at Odds Over Draft Plan to Secure Critical Infrastructure," Federal News Radio, November 4, 2013, http://www.federalnewsradio.com/473/3497578/Industry-DHS-at-odds-over-draft-plan-to-securecritical-infrastructure).

[62] HSPD 7 gave primary responsibility for coordinating R&D to the Office of Science and Technology Policy.

[63] HSPD 7 did not describe specific responsibilities of the Intelligence Community, the General Services Administration, or the Federal Communications Commission.

[64] The White House, "Executive Order on Improving Critical Infrastructure Cybersecurity" Press Release, February 12, 2013, http://www.whitehouse.gov/the-press-office/2013/02/12/executive-order-improving-critical-infrastructurecybersecurity-0 (describing Executive Order as a "down-payment on expected further legislative action").

[65] 343 U.S. 579, 634 (1952).

[66] See also Government Accountability Office, Federal Laws, Regulations, and Mandatory Standards.

[67] The existing regulatory frameworks discussed here do not constitute an exhaustive list of all regulations applicable to critical infrastructure, but are only intended to provide some context for the following discussions.

[68] P.L. 109-295, §550 (codified at 6 U.S.C. §121 note). For a more detailed discussion of CFATS, see CRS Report R41642, Chemical Facility Security: Issues and Options for the 112th Congress, by Dana A. Shea.

[69] 46 U.S.C. §§70102-70103.

[70] E.O. 13636, §10.

[71] E.O. 13636, §9(a).

[72] See, e.g., 6 U.S.C. §121(d)(2) (directing the Secretary to carry out comprehensive assessments of the vulnerabilities of the key resources and critical infrastructure of the United States to determine the risks posed by particular types of terrorist attacks).

[73] U.S. Constitution, article I, §2, clause 1 ("[the President] may require the Opinion, in writing, of the principal Officer in each of the executive Departments, upon any Subject relating to the Duties of their respective Office").

[74] See, e.g., S. 3414 §104(c)(1) (112th Cong.) (barring the award of punitive damages against any regulated entity arising out of a cyber-incident if the entity is in substantial compliance with voluntary cybersecurity practices established under the bill). Exposure to civil liability may also be increased if an entity receives information about a cyberthreat (as under §4 of the Executive Order) and fails to take reasonable measures to defend against or mitigate that threat.

[75] See Restatement (Third) of Torts: Product Liability §4 (b) ("[a] product's compliance with an applicable product safety statute or administrative regulation is properly considered in determining whether the product is defective with respect to the risks sought to be reduced by the statute or regulation").

[76] E.O. 13636, §8(d) (Feb. 12, 2013). When developing the incentives, the Secretary is required to note "whether the incentives would require legislation or can be provided under existing law and authorities."

[77] See, e.g., Burmaster v. Gravity Drainage Dist. No. 2, 448 So. 2d 162, 164 (La. Ct. App. 1984) (Occupational Safety and Health Act regulations and standards published by industry groups warrant consideration as evidence of standard of care, even if they are not controlling).

[78] For more information on the current legislative framework for cybersecurity, including discussion of provisions in legislative proposals in the 112th and 113th Congresses, see CRS Report R42114, Federal Laws Relating to Cybersecurity: Overview of Major Issues, Current Laws, and Proposed Legislation, by Eric A. Fischer.

[79] House Republican Cybersecurity Task Force, Recommendations of the House Republican Cybersecurity Task Force, October 5, 2011, http://thornberry.house.gov/UploadedFiles/CSTF_Final_Recommendations.pdf.

[80] See, for example, The White House, "H.R. 624—Cyber Intelligence Sharing and Protection Act," Statement of Administration Policy, April 16, 2013, http://www.whitehouse.gov/sites/default/files/omb/legislative/sap/113/ saphr624r_20130416.pdf.

[81] See, for example, Jack Whitsitt, "Framing the Future," CForum, December 5, 2014, http://cyber.securityframework.org/blog/11/entry-10-framing-the-future/.

[82] See, for example, Paul Rosenzweig and David Inserra, Obama's Cybersecurity Executive Order Falls Short, Issue Brief #3852, February 14, 2013, http://www.heritage.org/research/reports/2013/02/obama-s-cybersecurity-executiveorder-falls-short; Dave Frymier, "The Cyber Security Executive Order Is Not Enough," Innovation Insights: Wired.com, March 1, 2013, http://www.wired.com/insights/2013/03/the-cyber-security-executive-order-is-not-enough/.

[83] For example, some suppliers to the federal government have reportedly called for suspension of procurement rulemaking relating to cybersecurity until the framework has been published (Aliya Sternstein, "Contractors Ask GSA to Freeze Cyber-Related Regulations," Nextgov, May 17, 2013, http://www.nextgov.com/cybersecurity/2013/05/ contractors-ask-gsa-freeze-cyber-related-regulations/63244/?oref=nextgov_cybersecurity).

[84] John Reosti, "Feds Leaning Toward Incentives to Boost Cyber Security Framework," Credit Union Journal, November 14, 2014, http://www.cujournal.com/news/feds-leaning-toward-incentives-to-boost-cyber-securityframework-1023493-1.html.

[85] For example, some believe that the framework, while voluntary, "could develop in such a way that companies will be forced to adopt prescriptive standards due to the fact that information on program adoption for 'high risk' industries may be made public. More concerning, this could be done without a review process and could be used to leverage [sic] in ways that may not be beneficial to lowering overall risk" (Testimony of David E. Kepler, Senate Committee on Homeland Security and Governmental Affairs and Senate Committee on Commerce, Science, and Transportation, "The Cybersecurity Partnership Between the Private Sector and Our Government: Protecting Our National and Economic Security," hearing, March 7, 2013, http://www.hsgac.senate.gov/hearings/the-cybersecurity-partnership-between-theprivate-sector-and-our-government-protecting-our-national-and-economic-security). See also Homeland Security News Wire, "Cybersecurity Business Cyberwarfare Critical Infrastructure," March 3, 2014, http://www.homelandsecuritynewswire.com/dr20140303-nist-s-voluntary-cybersecurity-framework-may-be-regardedas-de-facto-mandatory.

[86] Mike McConnell et al., The Cybersecurity Executive Order (Booz Allen Hamilton, April 26, 2013), http://www.boozallen.com/media/file/BA13-051CybersecurityEOVP.pdf.

[87] Testimony of Roger Mayer, House Committee on Energy and Commerce, "Cyber Threats and Security Solutions," hearing, May 21, 2013, http://energycommerce.house.gov/hearing/cyber-threats-and-security-solutions.

[88] The Government Accountability Office (GAO) expressed similar concerns about DHS's National Critical Infrastructure Prioritization Program (NCIPP) list of highest-priority U.S. infrastructure (Government Accountability Office, Critical Infrastructure Protection: DHS List of Priority Assets Needs to Be Validated and Reported to Congress, GAO-13-296, March 2013, http://www.gao.gov/assets/660/653300.pdf). The relationship between the NCIPP list and that under the executive order has raised some concerns. There appear to be some differences between the lists that have resulted in some disagreements with the private sector (see, for example, Testimony of Dave McCurdy, House Committee on Energy and Commerce, Cyber Threats and Security Solutions, hearing, May 21, 2013, http://energy commerce.house.gov/hearing/cyber-threats-and-security-solutions).

[89] See, for example, PricewaterhouseCoopers, "Why You Should Adopt the NIST Cybersecurity Framework," May 9, 2014, http://www.pwc.com/en_US/us/increasing-it-effectiveness/publications/assets/adopt-the-nist.pdf; Luis A. Aguilar, "Boards of Directors, Corporate Governance and Cyber-Risks: Sharpening the Focus" (presented at the Cyber Risks and the Boardroom, New York Stock Exchange, New York, NY: Securities and Exchange Commission, 2014), http://www.sec.gov/News/Speech/ Detail/Speech/1370542057946#. VI8v-8kXMo0; Paul A. Ferrillo and Tom Conkle, "Guest Post: Cybersecurity and Cyber Governance: Understanding and Implementing the NIST Cybersecurity Framework," The D&O Diary, August 13, 2014, http://www.dandodiary.com/2014/08/articles/uncategorized/guest post-cybersecurity-and-cyber-governance-understanding-and-implementing-the-nist-cybersecurity-framework/.

[90] National Institute of Standards and Technology, "RFI—Framework for Reducing Cyber Risks to Critical Infrastructure," October 23, 2014, http://csrc.nist.gov/cyberframework/rfi_comments_10_2014.html.

In: Cyberspace Threat Landscape
Editor: Cody L. Barker
ISBN: 978-1-63482-338-8

Chapter 4

INFORMATION SECURITY: AGENCIES NEED TO IMPROVE CYBER INCIDENT RESPONSE PRACTICES*

United States Government Accountability Office

WHY GAO DID THIS STUDY

The number of cyber incidents reported by federal agencies increased in fiscal year 2013 significantly over the prior 3 years (see figure). An effective response to a cyber incident is essential to minimize any damage that might be caused. DHS and US-CERT have a role in helping agencies detect, report, and respond to cyber incidents.

GAO was asked to review federal agencies' ability to respond to cyber incidents. To do this, GAO reviewed the extent to which (1) federal agencies are effectively responding to cyber incidents and (2) DHS is providing cybersecurity incident assistance to agencies. To do this, GAO used a statistical sample of cyber incidents reported in fiscal year 2012 to project whether 24 major federal agencies demonstrated effective response activities. In addition, GAO evaluated incident response policies, plans, and procedures at 6 randomly-selected federal agencies to determine adherence to federal guidance. GAO also examined DHS and US-CERT policies, procedures, and

* This is an edited, reformatted and augmented version of a United States Government Accountability Office publication, No. GAO-14-354, dated April 2014.

practices, and surveyed officials from the 24 federal agencies on their experience receiving incident assistance from DHS.

What GAO Recommends

GAO is making recommendations to OMB and DHS to address incident response practices governmentwide, particularly in CyberStat meetings with agencies; to the heads of six agencies to strengthen their incident response policies, plans, and procedures; and to DHS to establish measures of effectiveness for the assistance USCERT provides to agencies. The agencies generally concurred with GAO's recommendations.

What GAO Found

Twenty-four major federal agencies did not consistently demonstrate that they are effectively responding to cyber incidents (a security breach of a computerized system and information). Based on a statistical sample of cyber incidents reported in fiscal year 2012, GAO projects that these agencies did not completely document actions taken in response to detected incidents in about 65 percent of cases (with 95 percent confidence that the estimate falls between 58 and 72 percent). For example, agencies identified the scope of an incident in the majority of cases, but frequently did not demonstrate that they had determined the impact of an incident. In addition, agencies did not consistently demonstrate how they had handled other key activities, such as whether preventive actions to prevent the reoccurrence of an incident were taken. Although all 6 selected agencies that GAO reviewed in depth had developed parts of policies, plans, and procedures to guide their incident response activities, their efforts were not comprehensive or fully consistent with federal requirements. In addition, the Office of Management and Budget (OMB) and the Department of Homeland Security (DHS) conduct CyberStat reviews, which are intended to help federal agencies improve their information security posture, but the reviews have not addressed agencies' cyber incident response practices. Without complete policies, plans, and procedures, along with appropriate oversight of response activities, agencies face reduced assurance that they can effectively respond to cyber incidents.

DHS and a component, the United States Computer Emergency Readiness Team (US-CERT), offer services that assist agencies in preparing to handle cyber incidents, maintain awareness of the current threat environment, and deal with ongoing incidents. Officials from the 24 agencies GAO surveyed said that they were generally satisfied with the assistance provided, and made suggestions to make the services more useful, such as improving reporting requirements. Although US-CERT receives feedback from agencies to improve its services, it has not yet developed performance measures for evaluating the effectiveness of the assistance it provides to agencies. Without results-oriented performance measures, US-CERT will face challenges in ensuring it is effectively assisting federal agencies with preparing for and responding to cyber incidents.

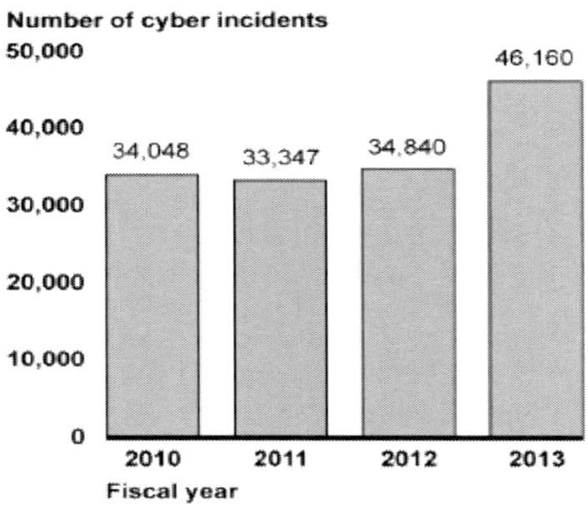

Source: GAO analysis of US-CERT data for fiscal years 2010-2013.

Cyber Incidents Reported by All Federal Agencies to US-CERT, Fiscal Years 2010-2013.

ABBREVIATIONS

DHS	Department of Homeland Security
DOE	Department of Energy
DOJ	Department of Justice
DOT	Department of Transportation
FISMA	Federal Information Security Management Act of 2002
FNR	Federal Network Resilience
HUD	Housing and Urban Development

NASA	National Aeronautics and Space Administration
NIST	National Institute of Standards and Technology
SP	special publication
US-CERT	United States Computer Emergency Readiness Team
VA	Department of Veterans Affairs

April 30 2014

The Honorable Thomas R. Carper
Chairman

The Honorable Tom Coburn, M.D.
Ranking Member
Committee on Homeland Security
and Governmental Affairs
United States Senate

The Honorable Susan M. Collins
United States Senate

Cyber-based attacks on federal systems have become not only more numerous and diverse but also more damaging and disruptive. Protecting the information systems and the information that resides on them and effectively responding to a cyber incident[1] is important to federal agencies because the unauthorized disclosure, alteration, and destruction of the information on those systems can result in great harm to those involved.

According to the National Institute of Standards and Technology (NIST), 2 preventive activities developed from the results of a risk assessment can help federal agencies and other entities to deter known cybersecurity[3] threats and to respond to them quickly. Having policies, plans, and procedures in place to guide agencies in responding to a cyber incident is critically important to minimizing loss and destruction, mitigating the weaknesses that have been exploited, and restoring IT services.

The *Federal Information Security Management Act of 2002* (FISMA)[4] requires agencies to develop, document, and implement an information security program. FISMA also authorizes the establishment of a federal information security incident center to assist agencies in handling a cyber incident. The Office of Management and Budget (OMB) has transferred certain information security responsibilities to the Department of Homeland Security (DHS).[5] Further, one of DHS's components, the United States Computer Emergency Readiness Team (US-CERT) operates the federal information security incident center required under FISMA.

You asked us to review federal agencies' ability to respond to cyber incidents. Our objectives were to evaluate the extent to which (1) federal agencies are effectively responding to cyber incidents and (2) the Department of Homeland Security provides cyber incident assistance to agencies.

To evaluate the extent to which federal agencies are effectively responding to cyber incidents, we randomly selected 40 incidents from each of 6 randomly selected[6] agencies: the Departments of Energy (DOE), Justice (DOJ), Housing and Urban Development (HUD), Transportation (DOT), Veterans Affairs (VA), and the National Aeronautics and Space Administration (NASA). We reviewed documentation related to the 240 incidents to determine the extent to which the agencies had performed cyber incident response activities in accordance with federal requirements and guidance and their own policies and procedures. This statistical sample allowed us to project the results, with 95 percent confidence, to the 24 major agencies[7] covered by the *Chief Financial Officers Act*.[8] We also reviewed the 6 selected agencies' incident response policies, plans, and procedures in depth and compared them to federal requirements and guidelines and interviewed officials from the selected agencies regarding their practices for responding to cyber incidents. We also administered a web-based survey to officials at the 24 major federal agencies to gather information about their incident response practices.

To evaluate the extent to which DHS provides cyber incident assistance to agencies, we examined DHS's policies, procedures, and practices. We reviewed agencies' survey responses for information about the type, quality, and usefulness of incident response guidance and services provided by DHS and US-CERT. We also interviewed DHS officials regarding their roles, responsibilities, and actions in assisting agencies in responding to cyber incidents.

We conducted this performance audit from February 2013 to April 2014 in accordance with generally accepted government auditing standards. Those standards require that we plan and perform the audit to obtain sufficient, appropriate evidence to provide a reasonable basis for our findings and conclusions based on our audit objectives. We believe that the evidence obtained provides a reasonable basis for our findings and conclusions based on our audit objectives. See appendix I for additional details on our scope and methodology.

BACKGROUND

A cyber incident can occur under many circumstances and for many reasons. It can be inadvertent, such as from the loss of an electronic device, or deliberate, such as from the theft of a device, or a cyber-based attack by a malicious individual or group, agency insiders, foreign nation, terrorist, or other adversary. Incidents have been reported at a wide range of public- and private-sector institutions, including federal, state, and local government agencies; educational institutions; hospitals and medical facilities; financial institutions; information resellers; retailers; and other types of businesses.

Protecting federal systems and the information on them is essential because the loss or unauthorized disclosure or alteration of the information can lead to serious consequences and can result in substantial harm to individuals and the federal government. Specifically, ineffective protection of IT systems and information can result in

- threats to national security, economic well-being, and public health and safety;
- loss or theft of resources, including money and intellectual property;
- inappropriate access to and disclosure, modification, or destruction of sensitive information;
- use of computer resources for unauthorized purposes or to launch an attack on other computer systems;
- damage to networks and equipment;
- loss of public confidence; and
- high costs for remediation.

While some cyber incidents can be resolved quickly and at minimal cost, others may go unresolved and incur exorbitant costs.

Thousands of Cyber Incidents Occur at Agencies Each Year

Reported attacks and unintentional incidents involving federal systems such as those involving data loss or theft, computer intrusions, and privacy breaches underscore the importance of having strong security practices in place. In fiscal year 2013, US-CERT received notifications of 46,160 cyber incidents at all agencies and 43,931 incidents at the 24 major agencies.[9] Cyber incidents reported by federal agencies increased in fiscal year 2013 significantly over the prior 3 years (see fig. 1), increasing almost 33 percent in the last 2 fiscal years.

The following examples reported in 2013 illustrate that information and assets remain at risk.

- July 2013: Hackers stole a variety of personally identifiable information on more than 104,000 individuals from a Department of Energy system. Types of data stolen included Social Security numbers, birth dates and locations, bank account numbers, and security questions and answers. According to the department's Inspector General, the combined costs of assisting affected individuals and lost productivity—due to federal employees being granted administrative leave to correct issues stemming from the breach—could be more than $3.7 million.[10]
- June 2013: Edward Snowden, an employee of a contractor of the National Security Agency, disclosed classified documents through the media. In January 2014, the Director of National Intelligence testified, in his annual worldwide threat assessment, that insider threats will continue to pose a persistent challenge, as trusted insiders with the intent to do harm can exploit their access to compromise vast amounts of sensitive and classified information as part of a personal ideology or at the direction of a foreign government.[11]
- June 2013: The Office of the Inspector General at the Department of Commerce reported that the department's Economic Development Administration inaccurately identified a common malware infection as a sophisticated cyber attack by another country. To remedy the situation, according to the Office of Inspector General, the Economic Development Administration spent more than $2.7 million—more than half its fiscal year 2012 IT budget—on unnecessary incident response activities and destroyed more than $170,000 worth of IT components officials incorrectly thought to have been irrecoverably infected. The Office of Inspector General reported that a failure to adhere to the department's incident handling procedures, a lack of experienced and qualified incident handlers, and a failure to

coordinate incident handling activities all contributed to the mishandling of the incident.[12]

- January 2013: A Romanian national was indicted in U.S. District Court for the Southern District of New York for allegedly running a "bulletproof hosting" service that enabled cyber criminals to distribute malicious software (malware) and conduct other sophisticated cybercrimes. Malware distributed by this hosting service had infected more than 1 million computers worldwide, including computers belonging to the National Aeronautics and Space Administration (NASA), causing tens of millions of dollars in losses to the affected individuals, businesses, and government entities. NASA's Office of Inspector General and the Federal Bureau of Investigation are investigating this incident.[13]

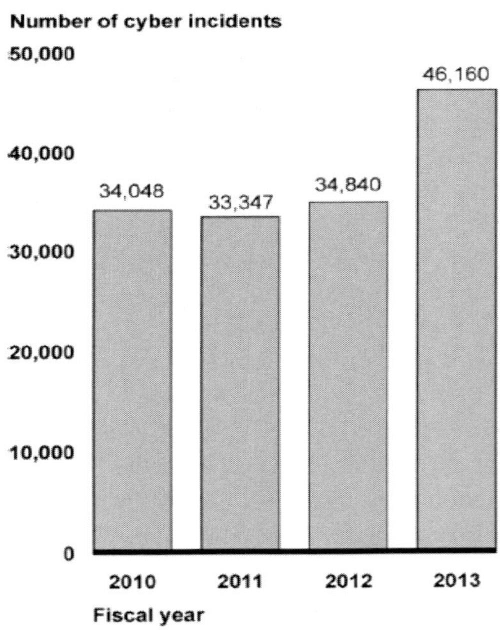

Source: GAO analysis of US-CERT data for fiscal years 2010-2013.

Figure 1. Cyber Incidents Reported to US-CERT by All Federal Agencies: Fiscal Years 2010-2013.

Federal Law and Policy Establish a Framework for Managing Cyber Risks

FISMA sets up a layered framework for managing cyber risks and assigns specific responsibilities to (1) OMB, including to develop and oversee the implementation of policies, principles, standards, and guidelines for information security; to report, at least annually, on agency compliance with the act; and to approve or disapprove agency information security programs; (2) agency heads, including to provide information security protections commensurate with the risk and magnitude of the harm resulting from unauthorized access, use, disclosure, disruption, modification, or destruction of information collected or maintained by or on behalf of the agency; (3) agency heads and chief information officers, including to develop, document, and implement an agencywide information security program; (4) inspectors general, to conduct annual independent evaluations of agency efforts to effectively implement information security; and (5) NIST, to provide standards and guidance to agencies on information security. Organized, planned cyber incident response activities are essential in defending an information system and the information that resides on it from an accidental or malicious cyber incident.

In addition, FISMA requires the establishment of a federal information security incident center to, among other things, provide timely technical assistance to agencies regarding cyber incidents. Each federal agency must also report annually to OMB, selected congressional committees, and the Comptroller General on the adequacy of its information security policies, procedures, practices, and compliance with requirements.

OMB and DHS Provide Oversight and Assistance to Agencies

In 2010, OMB transferred the operational aspects of its FISMA-mandated responsibilities for overseeing and assisting the cybersecurity efforts of federal agencies to DHS. Specifically, according to OMB, DHS activities are to include, but are not limited to:

- overseeing agencies' cybersecurity operations and incident response and providing appropriate assistance;
- overseeing the governmentwide and agency-specific implementation of and reporting on cybersecurity policies and guidance;
- overseeing and assisting governmentwide and agency-specific efforts to provide adequate, risk-based, and cost-effective cybersecurity;

- overseeing agencies' compliance with FISMA and developing analyses for OMB to assist in the development of the FISMA annual report; and
- annually reviewing agencies' cybersecurity programs.

Under presidential directive, DHS is also responsible for assisting public- and private-sector critical infrastructure owners and operators in preparing for, preventing, protecting against, mitigating from, responding to, and recovering from a cyber incident.

NIST Has Issued Federal Guidelines for Responding to Incidents

NIST has responsibility for developing standards and guidelines for securing the information systems used or operated by a federal agency or contractor on behalf of an agency. NIST has issued three special publications (SP) that provide guidance to agencies for detecting and handling cyber incidents.

NIST SP 800-61 specifies procedures for implementing FISMA incident handling requirements, and includes guidelines on establishing an effective incident response program and detecting, analyzing, prioritizing, and handling an incident.[14] The specific steps outlined for a formal, focused, and coordinated response to a cyber incident include a plan that should be tailored to meet the unique requirements of the agency and lay out the necessary resources and management support.

The incident response process that NIST outlines has four phases: preparation; detection and analysis; containment, eradication, and recovery; and post-incident activity. In preparing to respond to incidents, agencies should (1) develop and document policies, plans and procedures for appropriate incident handling guidance; (2) create and train an incident response team; (3) acquire the necessary tools and resources, such as those needed for analyzing incidents; and (4) periodically test their response capability to ensure it is working as intended.

Upon detection of an incident, analysis is needed to determine the incident's scope, such as affected systems, and potential impact to agency operations. These factors assist agencies in prioritizing response activities. In keeping with the severity of the incident, the agency can mitigate the impact of the incident by containing it and ultimately recovering from it. During this phase, activity often cycles back to detection and analysis—for example, to see if additional hosts have been infected by malware while eradicating a malware incident. After the incident has been managed, the agency may issue a report that details the cause and costs and the steps it should take to prevent a future incident. Policies, plans, procedures, as well as testing and training practices may require updates as lessons are learned throughout the various phases of response.

In addition, NIST SP 800-53 identifies specific incident response control activities that parallel those in NIST SP 800-61 and that agencies should address in order to effectively respond to a cyber incident.[15] These controls include, among others, (1) monitoring incident-handling activities (e.g., tracking and documenting incidents), (2) developing incident response policies and plans, (3) developing incident response procedures, (4) testing an agency's incident response capability, and (5) training incident responders.

NIST also provides guidelines on preventing malware [16] incidents and how agencies should respond to such an incident in an effective and efficient manner.[17]

US-CERT Provides Guidance for Reporting Incidents

Established in 2003, US-CERT is the federal information security incident center mandated by FISMA. US-CERT consults with agencies on cyber incidents, provides technical information about threats and incidents, compiles the information, and publishes it on its website, https://www.us-cert.gov/.

In addition, US-CERT defines seven categories of incidents for federal agencies to use in reporting an incident. Agencies are required to report incidents to US-CERT within specified time frames, such as within an hour or weekly or monthly, depending on the category of the incident. The categories and their time frames for reporting are listed in table 1.

Table 1. Incident Categories for Federal Agencies and their Reporting Time Frames to US-CERT

Category	Name	Description	Reporting time frame
CAT 0	Exercise/network defense testing	Used during state, federal, national, and international exercises and approved activity testing of internal/external network defenses or responses.	Not applicable; this category is for each agency's internal use during exercises.
CAT 1	Unauthorized access	An individual gains logical or physical access without permission to a federal agency's network, system, application, data, or other resource.	Within one hour of discovery/detection.

Table 1. (Continued)

Category	Name	Description	Reporting time frame
CAT 2	Denial of service	An attack that successfully prevents or impairs the normal authorized functionality of a network, system, or application by exhausting resources. Includes being the victim or participating in the denial of service.	Within two hours of discovery/detection if the successful attack is still ongoing and the agencyis unable to successfully mitigate the activity.
CAT 3	Malicious code	Successful installation of malicious software (e.g., virus, worm, Trojan horse, or other code-based malicious entity) that infects an operating system or application. Agencies are not required to report malicious logic that has been successfully quarantined by antivirus software.	Daily. Note: Within one hour of discovery/detection if widespread across agency.
CAT 4	Improper usage	A person violates acceptable computing use policies.	Weekly
CAT 5	Scans/probes/ attempted access	Any activity that seeks to access or identify a federal agency computer, open ports, protocols, service, or any combination for later exploit. This activity does not directly result in a compromise or denial of service.	Monthly Note: If system is classified, report within one hour of discovery.
CAT 6	Investigation	Unconfirmed incident that is potentially malicious or anomalous activity deemed by the reporting entity to warrant further review.	Not applicable; this category is for each agency's use to categorize a potential incident that is currently being investigated.

Source: US-CERT.

AGENCIES DID NOT CONSISTENTLY DEMONSTRATE EFFECTIVE CYBER INCIDENT RESPONSE PRACTICES

Based on our statistical sample of cyber incidents reported in fiscal year 2012, we estimate that the 24 agencies did not effectively or consistently demonstrate actions taken in response to a detected incident in about 65 percent of reported incidents.[18] Agencies frequently documented their incident response actions for containing and eradicating incidents, but did not consistently demonstrate how they had handled incident response activities for the analysis, recovery, and post-incident phases. Further, although the 6 selected agencies we reviewed had developed policies, plans, and procedures to guide their incident response activities, such efforts were not comprehensive or consistent with federal requirements.

Agencies Did Not Effectively Demonstrate Some Incident Response Activities

NIST specifies that agencies should document incident response activities, including analysis, containment, eradication, and recovery, as well as post-incident activities.[19] Although we found that agencies documented some required actions, they did not effectively demonstrate others.

Agencies' Demonstrated Aspects of Incident Analyses, but Did Not Complete Others

NIST SP 800-61 specifies that an initial analysis be performed to determine the type, nature, and scope of an incident, such as which networks, systems, or applications have been affected; who or what originated the incident; and what is taking place regarding the incident (e.g., what tools or attack methods are being used, what vulnerabilities are being exploited).

According to NIST SP 800-61, agencies are to consider impact for prioritizing incident response activities, such as the functional impact of the incident—the current and likely future negative impact to business functions. Resource limitations at agencies are one of the factors emphasizing the need for them to prioritize their incident response activities. Further, by prioritizing the handling of incidents, agencies could identify situations of greater severity that demand immediate attention.

The initial analysis of an incident should identify enough information for the team to prioritize subsequent activities, such as containment of the incident and a deeper analysis of the effects of the incident.

Agencies determined and documented the scope of an incident—a key part of the analysis—for about 91 percent[20] of incidents governmentwide.[21] Examples below illustrate both effective and ineffective scoping practices, such as:

- In a malware incident, the affected agency involved determined that after infecting a computer with malware, an attacker compromised the computer's local administrator account and used those credentials to successfully access another agency computer, which incident handlers then contained and remediated.
- In another incident, an agency received a report from US-CERT indicating that login credentials at two of the agency's components may have been compromised. When contacting the impacted components, agency incident handlers mistyped the potentially compromised credentials for one component and did not respond to an e-mail from the component requesting clarification, and failed to follow up with the second component when it did not respond to the initial alert. Despite these errors, the incident handlers closed the incident without taking further action.

In addition, most agencies did not consistently consider potential impact of incidents. Although the variance in our statistical sample was too great for us to project a percentage, 2 of the 6 selected agencies demonstrated that they had considered impact; the other 4 did not. In addition, 11 of the 24 agencies responding to our survey reported that they did not categorize the functional impact (e.g., low, moderate, and high) to their agency. Agencies risk ineffective and more costly incident response if they do not account for an incident's impact.

Agencies Demonstrated That They Contained the Majority of Incidents

NIST SP 800-61 states that an agency can minimize the impact of an incident by containing it, and emphasizes the importance of containing an incident before it overwhelms resources or increases damages. Containment strategies vary according to the type of incident. For example, an incident involving a lost mobile device could involve sending the device commands that will delete its data and permanently disable it, and then cancelling its access to mobile phone networks. A malware incident could be contained by physically or logically quarantining infected computers, preventing the malware from spreading over the network or communicating with the attacker who initially placed the malware.

Our sample indicates that agencies demonstrated that they had contained the majority of their cyber incidents. Specifically, our analysis shows that agencies had recorded actions to halt the spread of, or otherwise limit, the damage caused by an incident in about 75 percent of incidents governmentwide.[22] However, agencies did not demonstrate such actions for about 25 percent of incidents governmentwide.[23] For example:

- In an incident involving a lost iPhone, the device's mobile service was disabled before a "kill" command could be sent to the device, meaning incident handlers were unable to remotely delete e-mails and other data in its memory, potentially leaving the data exposed to anyone who found the device.
- In a malware incident, sensors on an agency's network recorded an agency computer contacting an external domain known to host malicious files, and downloading a suspicious file. Incident handlers closed the ticket without recording any actions taken to contain or otherwise remediate the potential malware infection.

Although agencies demonstrated that they had contained most of the incidents, those that were not effectively contained could increase the risk of the incident spreading and causing greater damage to their operating environments.

Agencies Demonstrated That They Eradicated Most Incidents

According to NIST SP 800-61, after an incident has been contained, eradication may be necessary to eliminate components of the incident, such as deleting malware and disabling breached user accounts, and identifying and mitigating all vulnerabilities that have been exploited. During eradication, it is important to identify all affected hosts within the agency so that they can be remediated. For some incidents, eradication is either not necessary or is performed during recovery. For example, after a lost mobile device has been remotely disabled and had its data deleted and network connectivity severed, incident handlers cannot take further actions regarding that mobile device. In the case of a minor malware incident, the malware could be removed from the system when the infected host has been removed from service or has had its hard drive wiped and its operating system and applications reinstalled.

Our sample indicates that agencies demonstrated that they completed their eradication steps for the majority of cyber incidents. Specifically, our analysis shows that for about 77 percent of incidents governmentwide, the agencies had identified and eliminated the remaining elements of the incident.[24] However, agencies did not demonstrate that they had effectively eradicated incidents in about 23 percent of incidents.[25] For example:

- In a malware incident, incident handlers noted that they had requested the creation of network blocks to isolate the infected computer and the collection of its hard drive for analysis, but the ticket had not been updated to indicate whether the incident handlers had performed the requested actions or any subsequent actions.
- After an administrative password was exposed to one facility's user population, incident handlers removed the password from the location where it had been posted, but did not indicate that they had changed the password to prevent users who had already seen it from using it.

Although agencies demonstrated that they had eradicated most of the incidents, those that were not effectively eradicated could increase the risk that components of an incident might still remain in the operating environment and cause damage.

Agencies Demonstrated Steps to Recover Systems, but Did Not Consistently Demonstrate Remedial Actions to Prevent Reoccurrence

According to NIST SP 800-61, in recovering from an incident, system administrators restore systems to normal operation, confirm that the systems are functioning normally, and (if applicable) remediate vulnerabilities to prevent a similar incident. Recovery may involve actions such as restoring systems from clean backups, rebuilding systems from scratch, and replacing compromised files with clean versions. NIST states that, during recovery, the agency should remediate vulnerabilities to prevent a similar incident from reoccurring (this could include, but is not limited to, installing patches, changing passwords, tightening network perimeter security, user education, adding or enhancing security controls, changing system configurations, etc.).

Agencies generally demonstrated the steps they took in restoring systems to normal operations. Specifically, our analysis shows that agencies returned their systems to an operationally ready state for about 81 percent of incidents governmentwide.[26] However, they had not consistently documented remedial actions on whether they had taken steps to prevent an incident from reoccurring. Specifically, agencies did not demonstrate that they had acted to prevent an incident from reoccurring in about 49 percent of incidents governmentwide.[27] For example:

- In a malware incident, incident handlers determined that a laptop belonging to an agency employee on travel was infected with malware, and was targeting other agency employees. While incident handlers contained the incident by quarantining the machine and blocking the remote sites it was communicating with, they noted that further actions could not be taken until the user had returned from travel. Incident handlers did not document what, if any, action, they took when the employee returned.
- In an incident involving the leak of personally identifiable information, the information of seven agency employees was posted on a third-party website. The data included name, addresses, phone numbers, partial credit card information, mother's name, e-mail addresses, and password. However, the agency did not document actions it took to determine how the leak had occurred, or how to prevent similar leaks from reoccurring. Incident handlers sent e-mails to the responsible component 31 times over a period exceeding 4 months, requesting status updates and confirmation that the component had taken remedial actions before the incident was eventually closed in the department's tracking system.

If incident recovery steps are not completed, agencies cannot be assured that they have taken all steps necessary to reduce the risk of similar incidents reoccurring and ensure that their systems will operate optimally.

Agencies Updated Policies or Procedures Post-Incident, but Did Not Generally Capture Cost Information

In its incident response guide, NIST states certain post-incident data can be used to improve the handling of future incidents. Lessons learned and reports from post-incident meetings can be used to update policies and procedures, such as when post-incident analysis reveals a missing step or inaccuracy in a procedure. Data such as the total hours of involvement and the cost may be used to justify additional funding of the incident response team.

After handling an incident, an agency should also issue a report that details the cost of the incident, among other information.

Agencies generally updated policies or procedures but did not consistently capture the costs of responding to an incident. Officials at 19 of the 24 agencies surveyed reported that their agency had amended policies or procedures as the result of a cyber incident. However, collection of cost data by agencies varied. Specifically, such information was recorded by only 1 of the selected 6 agencies we reviewed.[28] In addition, 12 of 24 agencies surveyed reported that they had captured the costs of responding to an incident. Without this information, agencies may be unaware of the costs of responding to an incident and lack the information necessary for improving their response in a cost-effective manner.

Selected Agencies' Policies, Plans, and Procedures for Cyber Incident Response Did Not Always Include Key Information

NIST states that, to facilitate effective and efficient incident response, agencies should develop corresponding policies, plans, procedures, and practices. However, selected agencies' policies, plans, and procedures did not always include key information.

Selected Agencies' Policies Did Not Include Key Information

NIST SP 800-61 states that policies are necessary for the effective implementation of a response to a cyber incident. Policies should identify the roles, responsibilities, and levels of authority[29] for those implementing incident response activities.

In addition, policies should address the prioritization of incidents, an activity that NIST deems to be a critical decision point in the process of handling an incident, and that handling should be prioritized based on factors such as the incident's impact to the organization. Agencies' policies should also address performance measures,[30] which can help evaluate the effectiveness of the incident response.

As shown in table 2, the six selected agencies' policies did not always address each of three key elements defined by NIST.

Table 2. Elements Key to Incident Response Policies at Selected Agencies

	Elements		
Agency	Define roles, responsibilities, and levels of authority	Prioritize severity ratings of incidents.	Establish performance measures
DOE	partial	no	no
DOJ[a]	partial	partial	yes
DOT	yes	no	no
HUD	partial	no	no
NASA	yes	yes	no
VA	partial	yes	no

Source: GAO analysis of agencies' incident response policies.
[a] DOJ's incident response policies are included within its incident response plan.

- **Roles, responsibilities, and levels of authority.** Policies for two of the six selected agencies addressed roles, responsibilities, and levels of authority for incident response. Specifically, DOT's cybersecurity policy tasked its Computer Security Incident Response Center with responsibility for implementing and monitoring incident handling for the agency and assigned roles for leading components' incident response planning to individual coordinators. Similarly, NASA's information security handbook specified the authorities of the incident response manager, who may, for example, decide to eradicate an incident without shutting down the system.
  Policies for DOE, DOJ, HUD, and VA partially defined the roles, responsibilities, and levels of authority for responding to cyber incidents. For example, while DOJ's policy defines roles and responsibilities, the agency did not include information on who had authority to confiscate equipment and did not describe when an incident should be escalated. In addition, VA's policies defined roles and responsibilities, but did not include authorities for the incident response team. HUD's policy addressed roles, responsibilities, and levels of authority, but the policy was still in draft at the time of our review. If levels of authority are not clearly defined, agencies risk ineffective incident response, since personnel may be unsure of their responsibilities in responding to an incident.
- **Prioritize severity ratings of incidents.** Policies for two of the six selected agencies fully addressed the prioritization of incidents. For example, NASA's handbook specified that, as part of prioritizing the

handling of an incident, the following should be considered: the incident's categorization, information sensitivity, the system's categorization, and the impact to the system or mission. Conversely, policies for DOE, DOT, and HUD did not address the prioritizing of incidents and DOJ partially addressed it. For example, DOJ's policy addressed the prioritizing of incidents affecting classified systems but not for unclassified systems. Agencies risk an ineffective response if they do not consider an incident's impact, since incidents having the most effect on an agency or its mission may not be addressed in a timely manner.

- **Establish performance measures.** One of the six selected agencies addressed the establishment of performance measures. DOJ listed several objectives for measuring incident response, such as limiting an incident's duration, minimizing impact to the department's operations, and requiring annual tests of the department's incident response capability. Policies for DOE, DOT, HUD, NASA, and VA did not address any measures of performance. Without such measures, agencies may lack the information needed to evaluate the effectiveness of their incident response.

Selected Agencies' Plans Did Not Address All Key Elements

NIST SP 800-61 states that incident response plans should be developed to provide guidance for implementing incident response practices based on the agency's policies. Further, NIST states the plan should be approved by senior management to indicate their support for the plan. The plan should also include and define metrics for measuring and evaluating the effectiveness of incident response. According to NIST, one such example would be "the total amount of labor spent working on the incident."

As shown in table 3, the six selected agencies' incident response plans did not consistently address two of the key elements defined by NIST. Following the table is a further discussion of those agencies' incident response plans.

Table 3. Elements Key to Incident Response Plans at Selected Agencies

Agency	Elements	
	Senior management approval	Metrics for measuring incidentresponse capability and effectiveness
DOE	yes	no
DOJ	yes	partial

Agency	Elements	
	Senior management approval	Metrics for measuring incidentresponse capability and effectiveness
DOT	no	no
HUD	no	no
NASA	yes	no
VA	yes	no

Source: GAO analysis of agencies' incident response plans.

- **Senior management approval.** Senior managers approved incident response plans for four of the six selected agencies. For example, DOE's deputy secretary approved the department plan, and DOJ's Chief Information Officer signed and approved his agency's incident response plan. Similarly, NASA's Deputy Chief Information Officer for IT Security approved the agency's document and VA's Network Security Operations Center Director also approved his department's plan. However, DOT's plan did not indicate that its senior management had approved it and HUD had not yet developed a plan at the time of our review. Without senior management commitment, an agency may not have the support for resources necessary to implement an effective incident response.
- **Metrics for measuring effectiveness.** Only one of the six selected agencies included metrics for measuring their incident response capability and effectiveness. To illustrate, DOJ's plan included requirements for reporting incidents within established time frames, for example, that a data loss involving sensitive information should be reported within 1 hour. However, other metrics listed on the plan were not measurable. We have previously noted that it is important to develop metrics that are measurable.[31] The remaining five agencies (i.e., DOE, DOT, HUD, NASA, and VA) did not address metrics in their incident response plans. If agencies do not include metrics in their plans, they may not be able to establish clear goals needed for measuring and determining whether their incident response is effective.

Selected Agencies Did Not Always Develop Procedures for Incident Response

FISMA requires agencies to develop procedures for responding to an incident. NIST SP 800-61 also states that, in addition to being based on incident response policies, such procedures should provide detailed steps for responding to an incident and cover all phases of the incident response process. According to NIST, following standardized responses as listed in procedures should minimize errors resulting from "stressful" incident handling situations. NIST lists several types of incident response procedures that agencies should develop. These include procedures for containing an incident that detail how incident handlers should contain specific types of incidents in a manner that meets the agency's definition of acceptable risk and procedures for prioritizing incident handling, which allow incident handlers to more quickly determine how best to apply their resources based on risk.

As shown in table 4, selected agencies did not always develop procedures for responding to incidents, as NIST suggests.

Table 4. Incident Response Procedures at Selected Agencies

Agency	Procedures for containing incidents	Procedures that address the prioritization of handling incidents
DOE	partial	partial
DOJ	yes	no
DOT	yes	no
HUD	yes	partial
NASA	yes	yes
VA	yes	yes

Source: GAO analysis of agencies' incident response procedures.

- **Procedures for containing incidents.** Five of the six selected agencies developed procedures for containing incidents. For example, DOJ developed procedures for handling e-mails with malicious content and procedures for blocking potential malicious IP addresses. Similarly, DOT's incident response group's standard operating procedures identify procedures for handling key logging software, which can record keystrokes and capture sensitive information such as usernames and passwords. However, DOE procedures partially addressed the containing of incidents. For example, while the department had not developed procedures for containing incidents, two DOE components had developed such procedures. Without procedures for containing incidents, incident response personnel may not have instructions necessary to prevent incidents from negatively affecting other parts of their operating environment.
- **Procedures for prioritizing incidents.** Two of the six selected agencies developed and documented procedures for prioritizing the

handling of incidents. NASA listed eight factors for determining the priority of handling an incident. Each of the factors is to be assigned a rating, after which the ratings for each factor would be added together to determine a number that would then be mapped to a priority ranging from low to critical. In addition, VA developed procedures for prioritizing incidents where a matrix would be used to map the type of incident to a predefined priority, such as critical, high, medium, and low, for handling the incident. Procedures for HUD and DOE partially addressed this activity since their procedures did not specify whether risk or impact would determine incident handling priorities. The remaining two of the six agencies (i.e., DOJ and DOT) had not developed and documented procedures for prioritizing incidents. As a result, these agencies may not be addressing incidents affecting the agency in the most risk-effective manner.

Other Incident Response Practices Were Not Implemented

NIST SP 800-53 states that agencies are to test their incident response capability, at an agency-defined frequency, for their information systems to determine the effectiveness of procedures for responding to cyber incidents. Agencies should also train personnel in their incident response roles and responsibilities.

According to NIST, the lack of a well-trained and capable staff could result in inefficient incident detection and analysis and costly mistakes.

As shown in table 5, agencies did not test their incident response capabilities or consistently train staff responsible for responding to incidents.

Table 5. Other Incident Response Practices at Selected Agencies

	Other incident response practices	
Agency	Tested incident response	Trained incident response personnel
DOE	partial	partial
DOJ	partial	yes
DOT	no	yes
HUD	no	yes
NASA	no	partial
VA	no	no

Source: GAO analysis of agencies' incident response practices.

- **Tested incident response capability.** Four of the six agencies had not tested their incident response capability and two—DOE and DOJ — partially tested their incident response capabilities. For example, DOE did not demonstrate that the department had conducted an entitywide test of its incident response capability and only provided information concerning a review of a key component's incident response activities. In addition, components at DOJ are responsible for testing their own incident response capability, with 10 of the 13 agency components completing testing of their capabilities. If an agency's incident response capability has not been tested, the agency will have limited assurance its controls have been effectively implemented.
- **Trained incident response personnel.** Three of the six agencies trained their incident response personnel. For example, both DOJ and HUD maintained a list of personnel who were responsible for responding to their department's incidents. These lists included the dates staff received training and the type of training received. DOT also trained their incident response personnel. However, VA did not demonstrate that their incident response personnel had received training, and DOE and NASA partially addressed this activity. For example, NASA provided a detailed listing of incident response personnel and the types of training they had taken, but did not define what qualified as acceptable training. If staff do not receive training on their incident response roles, they may not have the knowledge or skills to ensure they are prepared to effectively respond to cyber incidents affecting their agency.

OMB and DHS Have Not Used the CyberStat Review Process to Address Agencies' Incident Response Practices

Inconsistencies in agencies' performance of incident response activities and development of policies, plans, and procedures indicate that further oversight, such as that provided by OMB's and DHS's CyberStat review process, may be warranted. CyberStat reviews are in-depth sessions with National Security Staff, OMB, DHS, and an agency to discuss that agency's cybersecurity posture and discuss opportunities for collaboration. According to OMB, these reviews were face-to-face, evidence-based meetings to ensure agencies were accountable for their cybersecurity posture and to assist them in developing focused strategies for improving their information security posture in areas where they faced challenges. According to DHS, the goal for fiscal year 2013 was for all 24 major agencies to be reviewed. However, this goal was not met.

DHS officials stated that the reviews were conducted with 7 federal agencies, and that interviews were conducted with chief information officers from the other 17 agencies.

In addition, the current CyberStat reviews have not generally covered agencies' cyber incident response practices, such as considering impact to aid in prioritizing incident response activities, recording key steps in responding to an incident, and documenting the costs for responding to an incident.

DHS officials told us that, regarding incident response, the reviews discussed the status of agencies' closing of incidents and trends surrounding incident reporting; however, the reviews did not address evaluating the incident response practices of the agencies. Without addressing response practices in these reviews, OMB and DHS may be missing opportunities to help agencies improve their information security posture and more effectively respond to cyber incidents.

Agencies Were Generally Satisfied with Services Provided by DHS, but Reported That DHS Could Enhance Assistance to Agencies

While DHS provides various services to agencies to assist them in addressing cyber incidents, opportunities exist to improve the usefulness of these services, according to the 24 agencies we surveyed. DHS components, including US-CERT, offer services that assist agencies in preparing to handle incidents, maintain awareness of the current threat environment, and deal with ongoing incidents. Based on responses to our survey, officials at 24 major agencies were generally satisfied with DHS's service offerings, although they identified improvements they believe would make certain services more useful, such as improving reporting requirements. For its part, US-CERT does not evaluate the effectiveness of its incident services.

DHS Makes a Variety of Incident Services Available to Agencies

US-CERT serves as the central federal information security incident center mandated by FISMA. By law, the center is required to

- provide timely technical assistance to operators of agency information systems regarding security incidents,
- compile and analyze information about incidents that threaten information security,
- inform operators of agency information systems about current and potential information security threats and vulnerabilities, and
- consult with NIST and agencies operating national security systems regarding security incidents.

More broadly, OMB has transferred responsibility to DHS for the operational aspects of federal cybersecurity, including overseeing and assisting federal agencies' cybersecurity operations and incident response. Table 6 lists DHS cyber incident assistance services.

Table 6. Informational and Technical Assistance Services Provided by DHS to Federal Agencies

Service	Description
US-CERT portal	Provides a secure online forum for vetted incident responders to share information about cyber incidents, threats, and vulnerabilities.
US-CERT website	Provides alerts about new and ongoing attacks, links to information on newly identified vulnerabilities, contact information for US-CERT, and links and instructions for reporting incidents, phishing, malware,and software vulnerabilities.
Malware analysis	Analyzes agency-submitted malware samples to identify their functionality and behavioral characteristics, in support of improving detection and mitigation activities.
Digital forensics	Analyzes the current state of digital artifacts (e.g., computer systems, storage mediums such as hard drives, CD-ROM, and physical memory of computer systems using industry standard tools).
Einstein[a] alerts	Develops and deploys threat indicator signatures across Einstein 2 to improve detection capabilities. Monitors and correlates Einstein 1 and Einstein 2 sensor data to identify potentially malicious activity directed at agency networks and reports it to incident handlers.
Red team/Blue team	Provides services including assessments of agencies' technical cybersecurity capabilities, and operational readiness, vulnerability assessment and validation, testing of web applications, and testingof incident response capabilities.

Service	Description
On-site technical assistance	US-CERT analysts with specialized laptops and digital forensic data capture equipment provide on-site incident response to an agency.
Threat and vulnerability warnings	Review and correlate technical data from partners, constituents, and monitoring systems and use this information to develop periodical and event-driven alerts and warnings for US-CERT's partners and constituents.

Source: GAO analysis of DHS documents

[a] Einstein is a set of systems that monitor federal agencies' connections to the Internet. Einstein 1 allows agencies to monitor network traffic between their network connections and the Internet, while Einstein 2 has intrusion detection capabilities that can identify potentially malicious network activity as it is occurring and alert incident handlers. Einstein 3, which DHS is currently deploying, will include the capability to automatically block malicious traffic upon detection.

Surveyed Agency Officials Identified Opportunities to Improve DHS Incident Services

The results of our survey indicate that agency officials were generally satisfied with the services provided to them by DHS, and they offered various opinions about DHS services or noted dissatisfaction with incident reporting requirements. Of the agency officials that used services provided to them by DHS, as illustrated in figure 2, the majority were generally satisfied, finding the service to be very or moderately useful.

In addition, officials from 16 of the 24 agencies reported that they were generally satisfied with DHS's outreach efforts to inform them of cyber incident services and assistance, while 4 of the 24 officials reported that they were generally dissatisfied.[32]

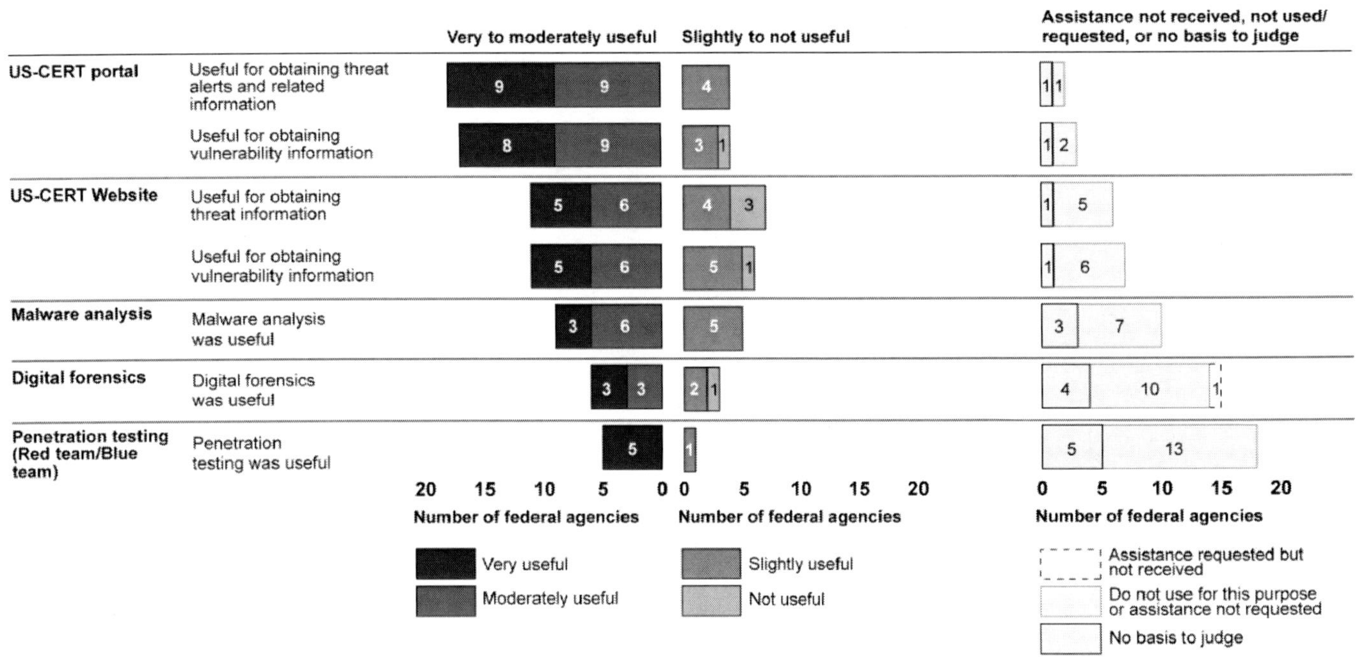

Source: GAO survey.

Figure 2. Satisfaction with Services Provided by DHS, as Reported by Agencies.

However, surveyed officials at 11 of the 24 agencies noted dissatisfaction with incident reporting requirements. Agency officials made the following comments:

- Time frames are difficult to meet.
- The incident categories are no longer practical. Attributes that contribute to classification are not unique between the categories and it allows for too much discretion and interpretation. The categories are long overdue for updates.
- A category that separates data loss from unauthorized access would be beneficial.
- A category specific to phishing and advanced persistent threats would be helpful.
- Add a category for non-incident. Additionally, each category should have sub-categories to further identify the incident and how it happened.

These comments are consistent with the results of a review we conducted in 2013.[33] Based on that review, we made recommendations to OMB to revise reporting requirements to DHS for personally identifiable information-related data breaches, including time frames that would better reflect the needs of individual agencies and the government as a whole. DHS officials provided information about actions the agency plans to take to help address our recommendations and stated that it has interacted with OMB regarding requirements specific to these recommendations and is preparing new incident reporting guidance for agencies.

US-CERT Receives Feedback to Improve Services, but Has Not Yet Developed Performance Measures for Evaluating the Effectiveness of Assistance Provided to Agencies

We and others[34] have noted the value of having clear performance measures that demonstrate results. Such measures support an agency's efforts to plan, reinforce accountability, and advance the agency's mission.

However, US-CERT has not established measures to evaluate the effectiveness of the cyber incident assistance it provides to agencies. USCERT gathers usage statistics and feedback on its public website and portal and uses those data to identify opportunities for improving those services, but it only performs these reviews on an ad-hoc basis. For its other activities, a US-CERT official stated that the agency gathers monthly statistics on activities such as the number of on-site or remote technical assistance engagements it performs each month, or the number of pieces of malware analyzed by staff.

The official noted, however, that these numbers are driven by factors outside of US-CERT's control, and as such, indicate activity levels rather than performance measures and that the agency is still trying to identify meaningful performance measures. However, without results-oriented performance measures, US-CERT will face challenges in ensuring it is effectively assisting federal agencies with preparing for and responding to cyber incidents.

CONCLUSION

With federal agencies facing increasing and more threatening cyber incidents, it is essential for them to be able to effectively manage their response activities. However, agencies did not consistently demonstrate that they responded to cyber incidents in an effective manner. Although agencies often demonstrated that they carried out various aspects of incident response activities, documenting all of the steps taken to analyze, contain, eradicate, and recover from incidents are important actions for agencies to take to ensure that incidents are being appropriately addressed. Having comprehensive policies, plans, and procedures that include measures of performance and guidance on impact assessment provide key elements necessary for agencies to effectively respond to cyber incidents. Testing the incident response program and ensuring employees are appropriately trained increases the assurance that controls are in place to prevent, detect, or respond to incidents. Further, capturing related costs could help agencies more efficiently manage their incident response activities. OMB and DHS have established CyberStat reviews to improve information security at federal agencies, but the reviews have not focused on agencies' incident response practices.

Although DHS and US-CERT offer numerous services to agencies to assist with cyber incidents, US-CERT does not have a process in place to evaluate the effectiveness of the assistance that it provides agencies. Without results-oriented performance measures, US-CERT will face challenges in ensuring that it is effectively assisting federal agencies with preparing for and responding to cyber incidents.

RECOMMENDATIONS FOR EXECUTIVE ACTION

To improve the effectiveness of governmentwide cyber incident response activities, we recommend that the Director of OMB and Secretary of Homeland Security address agency incident response practices governmentwide, in particular through CyberStat meetings, such as emphasizing the recording of key steps in responding to an incident.

To improve the effectiveness of cyber incident response activities, we are making 25 recommendations to six selected agencies to improve their cyber incident response programs.

We recommend that the Secretary of Energy:

- revise policies for incident response to include requirements for defining the incident response team's level of authority, prioritizing the severity ratings of incidents based on impact and establishing measures of performance;
- revise the department's incident response plan to include metrics for measuring the incident response capability and its effectiveness;
- develop incident response procedures that provide instructions for containing incidents and revise procedures for incident response to prioritize the handling of incidents by impact;
- fully test the department's incident response capability; and
- establish clear requirements to ensure the department's incident response personnel are trained.

We recommend that the Attorney General of the United States:

- revise policies for incident response by including requirements for defining the incident response team's level of authority, and prioritizing the severity ratings of incidents for unclassified systems, based on impact;
- revise the department's incident response plan to include quantifiable metrics for measuring the incident response capability and its effectiveness;
- develop incident response procedures that provide instructions for prioritizing the handling of incidents by impact; and
- ensure that all components test their incident response capability.

We recommend that the Secretary of Transportation:

- revise policies for incident response by including requirements for prioritizing the severity ratings of incidents based on impact and establishing measures of performance;
- revise the department's incident response plan to include senior management's approval, and metrics for measuring the incident response capability and its effectiveness;
- develop incident response procedures that provide instructions for prioritizing the handling of incidents by impact; and
- test the department's incident response capability.

We recommend that the Secretary of Housing and Urban Development:

- finalize policies for incident response and include in those policies requirements for prioritizing the severity ratings of incidents and establishing measures of performance;
- develop a departmentwide incident response plan that includes, among other elements, senior management's approval, and metrics for measuring the incident response capability and its effectiveness;
- revise procedures for incident response to prioritize the handling of incidents by impact; and
- test the department's incident response capability.

We recommend that Administrator of the National Aeronautics and Space Administration:

- revise policies for incident response by including requirements for establishing measures of performance;
- revise the agency's incident response plan to include metrics for measuring the incident response capability and its effectiveness;
- test the agency's incident response capability; and
- establish clear requirements for training the agency's incident response personnel.

We recommend that the Secretary of Veterans Affairs:

- revise policies for incident response by including requirements for defining the incident response team's level of authority, and establishing measures of performance;
- revise the department's incident response plan to include metrics for measuring the incident response capability and its effectiveness;
- test the department's incident response capability; and
- train the department's incident response personnel per the agency's requirements.

To improve the cyber incident response assistance provided to federal agencies, we recommend that the Secretary of Homeland Security:

- establish measures to evaluate the effectiveness of the cyber incident assistance it provides to agencies.

AGENCY COMMENTS AND OUR EVALUATION

We sent draft copies of this report to the six agencies selected for our sample, as well as to DHS and OMB. We received written responses from DOE, DHS, HUD, NASA and VA. The audit liaisons for DOJ and DOT responded via e-mail. However, OMB did not provide comments to our draft report.

Six of the eight agencies generally concurred with our recommendations. Five agencies (DOE, DHS, DOJ, HUD, and VA) concurred with all of our recommendations. NASA agreed with three of four draft recommendations and partially agreed with the fourth recommendation. DOT responded that the department had no comments. In cases where these agencies also provided technical comments, we have addressed them in the final report as appropriate. DOE, DHS, NASA, and VA also provided information regarding specific actions they have taken or plan on taking that address portions of our recommendations. Further, DHS, NASA, and VA provided estimated timelines for completion of actions that would address our recommendations.

NASA agreed with our three recommendations to revise its incident response policy, revise its incident response plan, and test the agency's incident response capability. In addition, it partially concurred with our recommendation that the agency establish clear requirements for training its incident response personnel. The Chief Information Officer stated that agency personnel were being trained in their response roles and responsibilities. He added that his office would define what qualified as acceptable training for incident response personnel and that his office would then update policy to reflect the need for focused incident response training. We believe these actions, if effectively implemented, will satisfy our recommendation.

Gregory C. Wilshusen
Director, Information Security Issues

APPENDIX I: OBJECTIVES, SCOPE, AND METHODOLOGY

Our objectives were to evaluate the extent to which (1) federal agencies are effectively responding to cyber incidents and (2) the Department of Homeland Security (DHS) provides cyber incident assistance to agencies.

To address our first objective, we reviewed the *Federal Information Security Management Act (FISMA)*, National Institute of Standards and Technology (NIST) *Special Publication 800-53 Revision 3, Special Publication 800-61 Revision 2*, Office of Management and Budget (OMB) OMB-06-19,[1] and United States Computer Emergency Readiness Team (US-CERT) guidance to determine the key steps agencies should address when responding to a cyber incident. We then used a two-stage cluster sample to identify a generalizable sample of incidents to review for compliance with key steps. First, we selected 6 agencies from the population of 24 major agencies covered by the *Chief Financial Officers Act*,[2] using probability proportionate to the number of cyber incidents those agencies had reported to US-CERT in fiscal year 2012, divided by 32,442—the total number of cyber incidents reported to US-CERT in fiscal year 2012—sampling without replacement. The 6 agencies selected were the Departments of Energy (DOE), Justice (DOJ), Housing and Urban Development (HUD), Transportation (DOT), Veterans Affairs (VA), and the National Aeronautics and Space Administration (NASA).

After selecting the 6 agencies in the first stage of sampling, we then obtained for each agency the list of individual cyber incidents for fiscal year 2012. From those lists, we then randomly selected 40 cyber incidents within each agency, for a total sample size of 240 cyber incidents.

This statistical sample allowed us to project the results, with 95 percent confidence, to the 24 major agencies. Table 7 lists the number of incidents in our sample in each of the six US-CERT-defined incident categories.

Table 7. Sample Cyber incidents by US-CERT Incident Category

US-CERT category	Sample incidents bycategory
Category 1 —Unauthorized access	69
Category 2 —Denial of service	0
Category 3 —Malicious code	66
Category 4 —Improper usage	45
Category 5 —Scans/probes/attempted access	32
Category 6 —Investigation	28
Total	240

Source: GAO analysis of US-CERT data.

Because we followed a probability procedure based on random selections, our sample is only one of a large number of samples that we might have drawn. Since each sample could have provided different estimates, we express our confidence in the precision of our particular sample's results as a 95 percent confidence interval (e.g., plus or minus 7 percentage points). This is the interval that would contain the actual population value for 95 percent of the samples we could have drawn.

To determine the reliability and accuracy of the data we used to develop our sample, we interviewed knowledgeable agency officials and reviewed related documentation on internal controls for US-CERT's database of incident tickets and reviewed the data for duplicates and outliers. For the incident data in our sample, we interviewed officials at the six agencies in our sample, reviewed each agency's incident management system to gain an understanding of the data, reviewed related documentation on internal controls for each agency's incident management system, and traced a random sample of records back to source agency documents and tested the fields for accuracy. Our sample results capture estimates for the extent of duplicate records, false positives, and inaccurately recorded data fields. Based on this assessment, we determined that the data were sufficiently reliable for our work.

To address the effectiveness with which agencies responded to a cyber incident, we reviewed documents (extracted from agencies' incident tracking systems) covering the incidents in our sample to determine the extent to which the agencies had performed analysis, containment, eradication, recovery, reporting, and post-incident procedures in accordance with federal requirements and guidance and their own policies and procedures. In addition, we reviewed and analyzed the six selected agencies' cyber incident response policies, plans, procedures, and practices and compared them to key elements in NIST guidance; and interviewed agency officials to discuss their incident response practices.

We also conducted a web-based survey of officials responsible for cyber incident response at the 24 major federal agencies.

After we drafted the questionnaire, we asked for comments from independent GAO survey professionals, and we conducted two in-person pretests to check that (1) the questions were clear and unambiguous, (2) terminology was used correctly, (3) the questionnaire did not place an undue burden on agency officials, (4) the information could be obtained, and (5) the survey was comprehensive and unbiased. We chose the pretest participants to include one member of our survey population, and one official from a federal agency not in our population, but who had a similar role and responsibilities with regard to incident response.

We made changes to the content and format of the questionnaire after the review and both pretests, based on the feedback we received.

We received completed questionnaires from all 24 agencies surveyed. Because this was not a sample survey, it has no sampling errors. However, the practical difficulties of conducting any survey may introduce errors, commonly referred to as nonsampling errors. For example, difficulties in interpreting a particular question, sources of information available to respondents, or entering data into a database or analyzing them can introduce unwanted variability into the survey results.

We took steps in developing the questionnaire, collecting the data, and analyzing them to minimize such nonsampling errors. For example, social science survey specialists designed the questionnaire in collaboration with GAO staff who had subject matter expertise. Then, we pretested the draft questionnaire with a number of officials to ensure that the questions were relevant, clearly stated, and easy to understand. When we analyzed the data, an independent analyst checked all computer programs. Since this was a web-based survey, respondents entered their answers directly into the electronic questionnaire, eliminating the need to key data into a database.

To address our second objective, we reviewed DHS documents, reviewed US-CERT's public-facing website and limited-access portal, and interviewed officials at DHS about the services it offers to agencies to support their incident response capabilities and activities. In addition, as part of our web-based survey, we asked officials at the agencies what incident response-related services or assistance they had sought from DHS, and their opinion of those services and the utility of US-CERT's public website and limited-access portal. In addition, we interviewed agency officials from the six agencies selected as part of our random sample regarding their interactions with DHS in receiving cyber incident assistance. We compared the assistance provided by DHS, including USCERT, to the requirements specified in FISMA. Further, we met with officials to determine whether the department had measures—such as those described by us and others[3]—to evaluate the effectiveness of the assistance they provided to agencies.

We conducted this performance audit from February 2013 to April 2014 in accordance with generally accepted government auditing standards. Those standards require that we plan and perform the audit to obtain sufficient, appropriate evidence to provide a reasonable basis for our findings and conclusions based on our audit objectives. We believe that the evidence obtained provides a reasonable basis for our findings and conclusions based on our audit objectives.

End Notes

[1] A cyber incident is a security breach of a computerized system and information and, for the purposes of this report, has the same meaning as a computer security incident, which the National Institute of Standards and Technology defines as a violation or imminent threat of violation of computer security policies, acceptable use policies, or standard security practices. The terms information security and information security incident apply more broadly to any forms of information and systems.

[2] NIST provides technical leadership for the nation's measurement and standards infrastructure, including the development of management, administrative, technical, and physical standards for the security of information in federal information systems. NIST's 800-series of Special Publications focuses on research, guidelines, and outreach efforts in information system security.

[3] As used in this report, cybersecurity refers to the security of computerized information systems and the information maintained in them.

[4] Pub. L. No. 107-347, Title III (Dec. 17, 2002).

[5] Office of Management and Budget, *Memorandum for the Heads of Executive Departments and Agencies: FY 2010 Reporting Instructions for the Federal Information Security Management Act and Agency Privacy Management*, M-10-15 (Washington, D.C.: Apr. 21, 2010) and *Memorandum for the Heads of Executive Departments and Agencies*, OMB M-10-28 (Washington, D.C.: July 6, 2010).

[6] We selected 6 agencies from the population of 24 of the major federal agencies covered by the *Chief Financial Officers Act*, used probability proportionate to the number of cyber incidents the agencies had reported to US-CERT in fiscal year 2012, and selected without replacing the agency into the original population.

[7] The 24 major departments and agencies covered by the *Chief Financial Officers Act* are the Departments of Agriculture, Commerce, Defense, Education, Energy, Health and Human Services, Homeland Security, Housing and Urban Development, the Interior, Justice, Labor, State, Transportation, the Treasury, and Veterans Affairs; the Environmental Protection Agency, General Services Administration, National Aeronautics and Space Administration, National Science Foundation, Nuclear Regulatory Commission, Office of Personnel Management, Small Business Administration, Social Security Administration, and U.S. Agency for International Development.

[8] 31 U.S.C. § 901.

[9] During fiscal year 2013, agencies reported a total of 61,214 incidents to US-CERT, which were comprised of 46,160 cyber incidents and 15,054 non-cyber incidents. According to US-CERT, a "non-cyber" incident is one that involves the mishandling of sensitive information without a cybersecurity component, such as the loss of a hard copy record containing personally identifiable information. Cyber incidents are the focus of this report.

[10] Department of Energy, Office of the Inspector General, *The Department of Energy's July 2013 Cyber Security Breach*, DOE/IG-0900 (Washington, D.C.: Dec. 6, 2013).

[11] James R. Clapper, Director of National Intelligence, *Statement for the Record - Worldwide Threat Assessment of the US Intelligence Community*, before the Senate Armed Services Committee (Feb. 11, 2014).

[12] Department of Commerce, Office of the Inspector General, *Economic Development Administration: Malware Infections on EDA's Systems Were Overstated and the Disruption of IT Operations Was Unwarranted*, OIG-13-027-A (Washington, D.C.: June 26, 2013).

[13] National Aeronautics and Space Administration, Office of Inspector General, *Semiannual Report, October 1, 2012-March 31, 2013* (Washington, D.C.: Apr. 29, 2013).

[14] NIST, *Computer Security Incident Handling Guide*, Special Publication 800-61, revision 2 (Gaithersburg, Md.: August 2012).

[15] NIST, *Recommended Security Controls for Federal Information Systems and Organizations*, Special Publication 800-53, Revision 3 with updates as of June 1, 2010 (Gaithersburg, MD.: August 2009). Although NIST released an updated version of SP800- 53—NIST Special Publication 800-53 Revision 4, *Security and Privacy Controls for Federal Information Systems and Organizations* in April 2013, we used SP 800-53 revision 3 for this audit. We relied on the previous guidance based on (1) our analysis showing that, while NIST added optional incident response controls and control enhancements in SP 800-53 revision 4, the eight core incident response controls did not change between the two versions and (2) OMB granted agencies a 1-year grace period after publication of new NIST guidance before they must be in compliance with the updated guidance, so the requirements from revision 4 were not yet in effect.

[16] Malware refers to a program that is inserted into a system, usually covertly, with the intent of compromising the confidentiality, integrity, or availability of the victim's data, applications, or operating system or of otherwise annoying or disrupting the victim's system.

[17] NIST, *Guide to Malware Incident Prevention and Handling*, Special Publication 800-83 (Gaithersburg, Md.: November 2005).

[18] Based on our sample, we are 95 percent confident that the estimate falls between 58 percent and 72 percent. This estimate represents the percentage of incident cases where the agency did not complete and/or document incident response activities completed for each of the phases—analysis, containment, eradication, and recovery—where required to do so.

[19] NIST, *Computer Security Incident Handling Guide: Recommendations of the National Institute of Standards and Technology*, Special Publication 800-61, Revision 2 (Gaithersburg, Md.: August 2012).

[20] Based on our sample, we are 95 percent confident that the estimate falls between 85 and 95 percent.

[21] For purposes of projecting our sample, we are using the term "governmentwide" to refer to the 24 major *Chief Financial Officers Act* agencies. Small agencies were not included in our sampling population.

[22] Based on our sample, we are 95 percent confident that the estimate falls between 65 and 84 percent.

[23] Based on our sample, we are 95 percent confident that the estimate falls between 16 and 35 percent.

[24] Based on our sample, we are 95 percent confident that the estimate falls between 66 and 86 percent.

[25] Based on our sample, we are 95 percent confident that the estimate falls between 14 and 34 percent.

[26] Based on our sample, we are 95 percent confident that the estimate falls between 68 and 91 percent.

[27] Based on our sample, we are 95 percent confident that the estimate falls between 41 and 57 percent.

[28] The variance in our statistical sample was too great for us to project a percentage.

[29] NIST states that the policy should also include levels of authority; the authority of the incident response team to confiscate or disconnect equipment and to monitor suspicious activity; the requirements for reporting certain types of incidents; the requirements and guidelines for external communications and information sharing (e.g., what can be shared with whom, when, and over what channels); and the handoff and escalation points in the incident management process.

[30] For this report, the term "measures" and "metrics" are used synonymously.

[31] GAO-09-617, *Information Security: Concerted Effort Needed to Improve Federal Performance Measures* (Washington, D.C.: Sept. 14, 2009).

[32] The remaining four agencies did not provide an opinion.

[33] GAO-14-34, *Information Security: Agency Responses to Breaches of Personally Identifiable Information Need to Be More Consistent* (Washington, D.C.: Dec. 9, 2013).

[34] See, for example, GAO, *Effectively Implementing the Government Performance and Results Act,* GAO/GGD-96-118 (Washington, D.C.: June 1, 1996) and CMMI Product Team, *CMMI for Services, Version 1.3* (Pittsburgh, Pa.: Carnegie Mellon University, 2010).

End Notes for Appendix I

[1] Office of Management and Budget, *Memorandum for Chief Information Officers: Reporting Incidents Involving Personally Identifiable Information and Incorporating the Cost for Security in Agency Information Technology Investments*, M-06-19 (Washington, D.C.: July 12, 2006).

[2] The 24 major departments and agencies covered by the Chief Financial Officers Act are the Departments of Agriculture, Commerce, Defense, Education, Energy, Health and Human Services, Homeland Security, Housing and Urban Development, the Interior, Justice, Labor,

State, Transportation, the Treasury, and Veterans Affairs; the Environmental Protection Agency, General Services Administration, National Aeronautics and Space Administration, National Science Foundation, Nuclear Regulatory Commission, Office of Personnel Management, Small Business Administration, Social Security Administration, and U.S. Agency for International Development.

[3] See, for example, GAO, *Effectively Implementing the Government Performance and Results Act*, GAO/GGD-96-118 (Washington, D.C.: June 1, 1996) and CMMI Product Team, *CMMI for Services*, Version 1.3 (Pittsburgh, Pa.: Carnegie Mellon University, 2010).

INDEX

C

F

G

H

I

J

K

L

V

W

Y